The Solid Rock

(Other Ground is Sinking Sand)

OLIVE ROSE STEELE

All names have been changed and details of stories blurred to
protect people's privacy
Scriptural translations are taken from the King James Version of the Bible
Book cover photo by Jessica Hope Beatrice Laing
Author's photo by Patrick Buchanan

ISBN: ISBN-13: 978-1505591910
ISBN-10: 1505591910
Published in 2016
The Sold Rock
(Other Ground is Sinking Sand)
Includes bibliographical references

DEDICATION

The Solid Rock is dedicated to my elementary school teacher,
(Miss Sanson) who encouraged me at eleven years old, to write my
first story titled: *My Self as a Penny.*

My wish is for individuals who might not yet be conscious of "Self",
to be awakened to their true faultless "Self".

CONTENTS

ACKNOWLEDGMENTS

Grateful thanks to the people who allowed me to tell their stories; each story is pertinent to the narrative of *The Solid Rock*. To my daughter Sharon for reminding me that inspirational interchange is what I'm good at. Her clear-sightedness pinpoints my ability to put forward common-sense understanding of truth. To my granddaughters, Jessica (Princess) and Gabriella (Precious), who've told me, as often as I produce a new book, how proud they are of me. To readers who've boldly alerted me of their hunger for more of my inspiring words; thanks for the vote of confidence. Many thanks to Cheryl Antao-Xavier for her assistance with copy editing *The Solid Rock*. And, as always, thanks to my husband for letting me be me. Be inspired!

INTRODUCTION

I WAS WALKING through my neighbourhood park on a cool fall day when an old favourite song, regularly sung by my late grandmother, came into my heart:

My hope is built on nothing less / Than Jesus' blood and righteousness / On Christ the solid rock I stand / All other ground is sinking sand / All other ground is sinking sand.

And at that moment I was overcome with mixed emotions— love, joy, doubt, fear, resentment, animosity. It dawned on me that my spiritual base was shaky. I was, literally, standing on unsteady ground, and maybe... just maybe... someone else, in that very moment, might be experiencing emotions similar to mine and maybe, just maybe *that* someone needed to be aware of a spiritual position, to cope with his or her state of mind. And right away I knew my next book would be titled *The Solid Rock* (Other ground is sinking sand).

In *The Solid Rock* I write about doubt, fear, perseverance, determination and the importance of truth-telling. I give opinions and methods by which people may make positive life changes and find a stronger footing in times of doubt.

I highlight the common grounds on which folks stand at certain stages in their life and I write true stories as examples of tricky and uncomfortable surfaces (situations) to show when it might be time to move to steadier or higher ground. *Stuff* is a word I use regularly throughout *The Solid Rock*. I encourage readers to be honest about where they stand with their *stuff*. I ask them to give the reasons they stay in such uncomfortable places, and whether they're satisfied with the stability of the ground on which they stand.

Let me tell you what I mean when I mention 'stuff.' Stuff is physical and metaphysical; it is the mental clutter in our heads and the physical clutter around us; it is relationships, good and bad; it is negativity, ours and others'; it is bad attitude, ours and others'; it is prejudice born of hurt, malice or belief system; it is 'baggage' from our past that we lug around in life. All of us carry similar yet unique 'stuff'.

Part One is about my personal *stuff*. I show how *My Stuff* is not different from other people's *stuff*. All through *The Solid Rock*, readers will recognize references I make to my own stuff… this is my way of spotlighting the powerful influence our *stuff* has on us.

Part Two, is about *stuff* that might be germane to most folks. Hence, I call Part Two: *Your Stuff*. I tell anecdotes to capture the essence of real emotions and I share these emotions using simple themes—*love, happiness, fear, insecurity, anger, hate, jealousy*—all of the mixed emotions that people deal with day to day. I review these emotions through personal reflections, always mindful that the stories I tell are rooted in everyday living. I honour the feelings that may surge to the forefront from folks even as they absorb the stories.

Part Three, is about *Our Stuff*. I remind folks that all of us—you and I, deal with different versions of the same challenges. Here I show that *Our Stuff* goes beyond just *My Stuff* and *Your Stuff*. It involves the *stuff* of people we don't even know: other people's stuff that somehow morphs into our space and impacts our lives in a significant way. Here, again I tell stories of such challenges that put us on a guilt trip, feeling responsible for other people's *stuff*. I give examples of how our *stuff* intermingles with the *stuff* of others.

I honor and respect the feelings of the folks who tell their stories; and readers who might share some of the same feelings. Many of you may raise an affirming hand in response to a statement or a passage in this book—take heart, I raised my hand first.

Parts Four, and Five are about personal beliefs, spiritual practices and access to self-help resources. I give examples of negative self-talk, I exhort folks to identify such talk and quickly drive them away.

Throughout *The Solid Rock* I mention *Self*. What is Self? *Self*, is the divine part of you and I. *Self* might be symbolised by a personal connection with Divine Spirit (God). It is that part of us that says "I am". The phrase "I am" should always be followed by: good, happy, healthy, loving and whole. *Self* is the "I am" that folks ought to explore.

In conclusion, I challenge you, reader, to *literally* evaluate the ground on which you stand. I pose engaging questions for your benefit. I sincerely hope that as you work through the exercise, you will take a closer look at your stance on the *stuff* discussed in this book.

I share some of my personal prayers in the final pages of *The Solid Rock* and I encourage you to begin journaling your own prayers. What a powerful spiritual workout you will receive from this exercise.

The biblical quotes in *The Solid Rock* were taken from the *King James Version* of the Holy Bible although there are other relevant versions.

Olive Rose Steele
Canada.

PART ONE

My Stuff

My hope is built on nothing less / Than Jesus' blood and righteousness / I dare not trust the sweetest frame / But wholly lean on Jesus' name. On Christ, the solid rock, I stand / All other ground is sinking sand / All other ground is sinking sand.

—My Hope is Built on Nothing Less, *Edward Mote.*

"...I will put thee in a cleft of the rock, and will cover thee with my hand." Exodus 33: 22. Read the entire chapter of Exodus 33.

Rock bottom became the solid foundation on which I built my life.

—J.K. Rowling, Author.

HE SHOULD BE approximately three inches taller, good-looking, well-mannered and well-dressed. Those were the criteria for my perfect mate.

Didn't matter that my husband wasn't the lawyer my mother anticipated for me or he wasn't from the well-off family I dreamed of settling into; I married him anyway.

We have opposite personalities, he thinks he's quiet, I know he's not. I think I'm too loud, he agrees and yet he always gives me latitude to be *me*.

We make mistakes, some by ourselves and some together. We experience 'dashed' hopes but we never stop hoping. Twists and turns in both our lives fluctuate; people enter and leave our space; families love us and then vacate; we win together and lose together... it doesn't matter.

We have each other to blame when things go wrong and rejoice with, when things are not to our liking.

We are each other's help-mate; every time life turns us in a new direction, my husband reminds me that he'll never walk without me. Yes, we're still walking together, still wishing and hoping.

What a roller-coaster ride it has been thus far and through it all we're standing.

Mama said there will be days like these... there will be days like these, my Mama said.

What changed?

I admit to my share of dysfunction in our marriage relationship and I put aside unhealthy traits which could block our progress.

Dear God
Please forgive my impatience towards my husband
I confess I am angry, resentful, unloving, and
unforgiving today; take this unkindness from me and
give me gentleness; let me rise above my negative
emotions; let me see my husband as Your child in
need of love; make me a good wife, companion and
help-mate. I now release all my negativity towards my
husband, and cast this burden on Christ within and
go free. And so be it.
—*Olive Rose Steele*

My husband and I no longer accept, as true, that we're bound to life's demands—millstones around our necks. We promised each other to stand our ground every time our paths become difficult. The times when we cast blame now become ancient history. We forgive our self for accepting fault, and move to safer ground. We see challenges as lessons to be learned.

Life would be so beautiful if everyone could be nice and loving at all times. I can talk about my unloving self towards my husband because in spite of my fears, insecurities, resentments, anger, rage, bad attitude and foolish pride, I still stand my ground, by my husband's side.

Like many wives, I worry about my husband's health, finances, sexuality, integrity, priorities, and even his attitude toward me and many times I dismiss his challenges as stuff a man ought to deal with.

In as much as I want to *take care of* some of my husband's stuff and take a load off him, there are many things that only my husband can and should deal with—*his* stuff. And only when his stuff is *mixed in* with my stuff, do I make it my business. Otherwise, I let him handle his stuff!

My husband and I have our own set of values and emotions. Our experiences (good and not so good) might have something to do with our emotions.

I try not to be hamstrung by my feelings and emotions though I recognize my feelings might very well affect my present and future outlook.

Imagine seeing yourself in a mirror that constantly shows you not to your liking. That is how it is with my husband and me. He forces me to face my dysfunctional self and helps me to make adjustments to the stuff that is not right about me.

—And When We Pray, *Olive Rose Steele.*

8

I admit, I'm 'under construction'—a work in progress. This is a gradual development and I've come a long way, with a long, long way to go. With this in mind, I can say I'm in it for the long haul. It is my intention to endure, with my husband in tow. Here are some true facts about me; I'm strong-willed, forward-thinking, ambitious, and always striving for better. I make my personal governing rules and perhaps I'm too headstrong for my good. I have purchased and consumed stuff; I horded stuff that was of no value, and discarded stuff I should've kept. And to rationalize my addiction to stuff, I have often said I cannot change —it's just the way I am.

Having experienced the fear of rejection, the fear criticism and the fear of loss of love; and having withstood constant dogging by these fears, I was not convinced I would be contented without *My Stuff*. Would I be uncomfortable without *My Stuff*? Could I be a complete person without stuff? If I were going to be happy, healthy, loving and whole as I was created to be, then I needed to seek out stuff that was good for my soul. It occurred to me that there was more to life than the tangible stuff I hoarded and piled up. I made a sharp turn to soul restoration.

It is comforting to know that I have no need to go through life carrying unnecessary burdensome stuff. It is with delight and a lot of self-confidence that I pack and un-pack stuff as I proceed on my journey.

—And When We Pray, *Olive Rose Steele*

Shake, Rattle, Roll

During the period of my 'comeuppance', I frequently stood on wobbly stones, trudged through deep mire and climbed over huge rocks. The stuff I stored up became oppressive. Peace and happiness avoided me. I knew if I continued with the perceived drama, my heart would revolt. I considered the ground on which I stood and questioned whether I was losing my nerve. Church seemed like a comfortable place.

Then I reflected on the *stuff* I had accumulated in boxes, drawers, closets, the basement and under my bed; *stuff* that piled up in the garage and *stuff* I had forgotten in the shed. I reasoned those were *stuff* to be donated to a thrift store or be organized for a yard sale. I was uncomfortable, unsettled; not sure whether I was making right decisions. I was trembling and yet I held my stance. I prayed.

Dear God
I stand in your presence covered in dirt
My eyes are filled with dust from my own folly
I cannot see my way out of this mess
I cannot remember how I got this dirt on me
Guide me through this valley
Shake me loose and stand me up
Help me to grasp and understand my lessons
And make me glad once more
In Jesus' name I pray
Amen.
—*Olive Rose Steele*

I realized I needed to *stretch* my faith, hope for my good and love *my Self*, notwithstanding the arrogance and smugness which I had shown in the past. Yes, I needed to be armoured with Faith, Hope and Love.

Faith is my belief in a Higher Presence; I call that Presence God. Faith assures that my best days are ahead. Hope comforts me as I go through uncertainties and points me to a brighter tomorrow. Hope gives me courage to withstand my spiritual walk. Love assures my existence; love is the breath I take, love directs my path and lights my way, love is what I give without query, love is my connection to the love of others.

My ego stepped in and remind me of the cherished things I had lost, customary favours that deserted me, friends who shunned me, and loved ones who questioned my rationale. My ego insisted that I look out for myself; go back to the things I know and love, and fight for *stuff* that's rightfully mine. I was terrified.

Fear of every kind came over me—rejection, poverty, lack, ill health, loss of credibility; all of these fears showed up to scare me. Fear made me think only of negative outcomes. Trials and challenges seemed always at my heels. My thinking was messed up even though I knew my prayers would be my armour to protect me from the hard knocks of life. I was alone in my daily battles.

Fear persisted until I recognized fear's methods and intentions. I surrendered to Divine Spirit within for direction.

First, I prayed to be forgiven for staying at such an uncomfortable fearful place for as long as I did. Then, I prayed to be sustained at a place of peace and comfort. Afterwards, I thanked God for leading and directing me despite my unworthy self. For a time, I stayed still. I waited for direction. I needed to know that all would be well. I admit I had doubts while I waited. Many times, during my periods of doubts, Spirit within gently nudged me with timely favours—a reminder that faith is the key ingredient in those times. And so I gradually weakened the grip of fear by refusing to accept its negative undertones. Now I don't spend valuable time standing with fear on an unsound footing; I take stock quickly, figure out fear's motives, and reach for the solid rock.

Through some of my most challenging moments, loved ones who wished me well encouraged me to *believe in* myself. To be honest, those were times when I was the only one who believed in *me*—those were tough times. In those times I was tempted not to believe in myself or anyone else. It is not so easy to be inspired when things aren't working out. So I began to pay attention to my *Self*—what am I seeing? What am I hearing? What am I feeling? Where am I going? In moment by moment prayer, I ask the Divine for direction and guidance and I enjoy the times I spend in prayer—just being me! I learn to inspire myself.

The secret is to say the right words or phrases at the right moment. In my book *Great is Thy faithfulness (Insights for seekers of Self)* I wrote: "Words may be all you have to give; your thoughtful words may be the only encouraging statement that someone else has heard in a long time."

In times when it is difficult to find the right words, I acknowledge that such difficulties call for unbending faith in the unseen. It is then that I let go of everything I think I know and allow Divine Spirit to lead me to that higher rock.

I admit there were times when I could not find a single inspirational word to give, like the time when my brother lost his life in an unfortunate accident; or when my friend Helen was diagnosed with cancer; or when it was confirmed that my mother-in-law (whom I loved very much) had developed Alzheimer's disease. Even the time when a stroke put my best girlfriend in a wheelchair for the rest of her life. Those were some of the times when I did not know what good words to give myself. If you find it difficult to give inspiring words, even to yourself—take heart; others have had the same difficulty. It is alright to be at-a-loss for words at such times.

It is true, some people will resent the fact that you give good words and other people might want to influence what you say or make you hold back on good words. Know that the good words you give might be the only good words someone else has heard in a long time—so give good words. In those times when words are hard to come by, your feelings will show. You will use your manifested feelings to express the right sentiment.

Starting over is exciting!

This is new. It used to be that I was in control of *my* life, and everybody else's life if they let me. Now I'm skittish about getting involved in other people's business. This new way of walking through life gives me a good feeling—I'm totally wrapped up with me, myself and I—experiencing more of *Self* and less of my ego. In time past, life forced me into personal do-overs and I used to say I'm *back to square one*. And, I've had to go *back to square one* on numerous occasions. The experience taught me valuable lessons in surrender and made me a better person. Life will send folks *back to square one* to repay or be refunded, or even relearn a lesson. Know that life sends folks *back to square one* for their own good.

My constant refrain

My prayerful conversations are unlike the ones I have with family, friends, colleagues and even around the boardroom table. Quite often I talk with my Heavenly Father when I'm alone, when I go for a stroll through my neighbourhood park, always in the quiet of my heart. With the knowledge that I can approach Him anywhere I please and at any time, I fearlessly claim my status as a child of God.

I realize all of this may sound religious to some folks, and it should, for we were made solely to love and serve God. Everything else should be unimportant.

***

The times when I found myself standing at a place that was cold and uncomfortable, when it seemed like my husband and I were on the receiving end of each other's drastic life changes, I was determined to put up a façade. I accepted that the sand in which I stood was shifting faster than I could find a foothold, and fear, in every form that one could imagine, had taken over my senses so I prayed.

I have prayed long tearful prayers when I thought I needed comfort; when my mind was held up in cold, dark spaces; when I wanted a ray of sunshine in my life. I have pleaded in prayer to be rescued from recurring fears. My prayers were about me and what I sought for myself. In my state of want and need, I was passed over, and abandoned in crucial circumstances. I prayed for clarity. I asked for an open mind and perfect vision, but relief was slow in coming. Then one day I was prompted by Spirit within to put my prayers in writing. I thought the idea was strange. Me? Reveal my heart in writing? I said *not me*, for I'm not a writer. (I honestly thought I was 'cut out' to be a businessperson). But I was pushed and prodded by Spirit within until I answered the call.

Now here I am, recognizing more of who I truly ought to be; writing words that encourage folks to be truthful about *Self*; telling folks their best and most productive years are yet to come and declaring that it is never over until it is over.

***

I pray thru challenging moments; relish special spiritual connections, enjoy ceremonial rites (christenings, baptisms, marriages, etc.). I talk truthfully about my wishes, believing that everything I need to survive this life is already given to me. I admit there were times when I debated whether my prayers go unanswered because I am not good enough, holy enough, worthy enough; still I prayed, confident that the Invisible Ear heard my cries. I've prayed over and over, with tears streaming down my face, for specific desires to be manifested. And when my prayers were not answered in the way I expected, I've asked myself some critical questions: What was my state of mind while I prayed? Was I specific about my needs? How great was my desire? Was I trying to control the outcome while I prayed?

In moments when I'm of a mind to worry, I remind myself of the unconditional love of God and I breathe deeper; knowing that worries do not come from a heavenly place; worries come from a place of fear where negative thoughts and feelings reside.

I have said that prayer ought to be a continuous practice and since we live and move in a perpetual state of prayer then we should pay close attention to our thoughts, words, and actions as we pray.

I say, be wrapped up in your prayers; cry if you want to; know that your prayers are recorded in secret—the Unseen Higher Power is paying attention to every word you say. Know that every prayer is answered; just open your heart and allow your prayers to manifest in a perfect way.

Pray for folks who are ill, hungry and homeless; folks who've done you wrong and folks who love you. And give thanks for being whole and able to pray on their behalf.

Dear God,

Use me to bring comfort to others

Use the words I speak

Use my expressed feelings

Use my actions toward others to draw them to You

Let me say words that others need to hear

Let me do things that need to be done

Let Your beauty be seen in me

And let everything be to your honour and glory

Amen.

—*Olive Rose Steele*

What have I missed?

My desire is to be prosperous, valued, and loved; stuff some folks consider praiseworthy but still I felt not good enough. Consequently, I put my trust in human benevolence in the hope that stuff I yearn for would show up through my own willpower.

Merciful Father
I give you my thoughts
Let Your Holy Spirit govern my thinking
Fill my mind with hope and confidence
Give me insights into what is causing my doubts
Let me say encouraging words to my Self
Help me not to grumble and complain
Let my words build me up and not tear me down
Help me to cast my burden on You
As I wait patiently for my good
In Jesus Name I pray
And so be it.
—*Olive Rose Steele*

It is true, all of us want more of the good things in life, but we don't always know what is good for us. And like me you might bawl your eyes out when you realize what is truly good for you might be different from what you expected.

I learned to be patient when it looks like things aren't going my way; accept that what is mine will come to me in perfect ways at the right moment and acknowledge that stuff which is not for me will not come to me.

My personal humbling stories:

On a snowy day, some years ago, I stood in a long line outside of a department store in Toronto, waiting to have the vinyl I had purchased, autographed by the late Peter Tosh of the group, Bob Marley and the Wailers. While Tosh was signing my album, I said to him: *I love you.* He never responded or made eye contact—my love words meant nothing to him. Know that your 'love' words might not be reciprocal.

On another occasion, I travelled by plane and paid *big bucks,* to attend a conference, out of country, hosted by International Speaker and bestselling author, Dr. Deepak Chopra. At the end of his talk, I waited for forty minutes to get his autograph on one of his book. I handed him a copy of my manuscript: *And When We Pray.* I did make sure all of the ways in which his representatives could get back to me were written on my manuscript. No one ever got back to me.

At a women's conference in Toronto, I listened to the address of a Doctor of Divinity. Her talk was stirring. At the end, I caught up with her in the auditorium, greeted her and asked her to autograph one of her books. She signed the book and quickly walked away. Puffed up? I don't know. Was I expecting too much attention from her? Possibly. Sometimes, being humble means turned away from.

Every day, unbeknownst to us, we inspire other people by our words and actions. Many people would prefer not to *stand out* or be recognized for what they do or say. But people who are called to inspire and show empathy should take the time to acknowledge the folks who approach them. It could be that the closest some folks might get to someone of influence who inspires them might be a platform, many, many feet away. And the folks who get close may request an autograph. Those who have not had such an opportunity should be forewarned; they might come away feeling like they were just another numbered person in a crowd.

In a group conversation, a year ago, I was prompted by Spirit within to talk candidly about *My Stuff*. My openness drew the annoyance of one participant who chided that the session was not a place for revelations and admissions. I immediately schooled the participant in question about the benefits and richness of expressive conversations.

By talking about *My Stuff*, the other members allowed themselves to talk openly about their *Stuff*.

Know that folks can see through cover-ups. Recognize that folks will take advantage of a façade in good and not so good ways. And having recognized the façade, folks might turn away from the pretender.

Aim to be realistic.

In this Part 1, I talk about what I know about my *Self* even if what I know is just a segment of my life. Knowing *some things* about my *Self* reveals inner conflicts, subtle masks and a 'victim' mentality that trails me. Yes, knowing these *things* matures my character and illuminates the healthy, happy, loving *Self* that is the woman I am.

My prayerful conversations are unlike the ones I have with family, friends, colleagues and even around the boardroom table. Quite often I talk with my Heavenly Father when I'm alone, when I go for a stroll through my neighbourhood park, always in the quiet of my heart. With the knowledge that I can approach Him anywhere and at any time, I fearlessly claim my status as a child of God.

PART TWO

Your Stuff

I don't care if you are religious or not and I think the message is that at the end of the day, everybody has to mature and everybody has to heal and mend their own injuries, emotional injuries on their own pace
—Boris Kodjoe, *Actor.*

If you haven't touched your own pain, you are just postponing the inevitable. It is only a matter of time before you have to acknowledge to yourself, if not to others, your dirty laundry: your judgments, your fears, your neediness, your suicidal thoughts.
—I am the Door, *Paul Ferrini.*

YOUR STUFF IS what you build up to keep your life moving along smoothly. Wealth, property, belongings and attire might be some of your noticeable stuff. Your stuff could be your pain, loss, hopelessness, disappointments and despair. And still, your stuff might be your thoughts, words and actions. You may accept as true that the stuff *you* own is what can make you happy; as well, other people may feel like they 'know' you just by observing the fundamentals of your stuff. That's how strong stuff is.

Theoretically, gather up your stuff—including your hopes and dreams; your doubts and fears; put them in a pile in your mind, now label the pile: *This is my life.*

Take an inventory of your pile of stuff, ask yourself: is my stuff serving me well? Am I truly happy with my stuff? Could I live without some of my stuff? Is my stuff weighing me down? Am I sure I have the right stuff? Do I know what is lacking? Now, ask yourself these *soul* questions: Am I standing on solid footing, wobbly stones, sinking sand? Am I between a rock and a hard place? Why am I where I am?

You should know that to be truly happy you need to accumulate stuff that nourishes your body and soul.

Okay. You may not be happy with your stuff (lifestyle). You are probably rethinking your routine after a divorce, a devastating financial meltdown, loss of your home to foreclosure, your car repossessed, and a sudden illness that threw a *monkey wrench* into your plans. The conundrum leaves a void. You think this might be the right time to turn over a new leaf although you're not ready to make drastic changes. Ask yourself these questions: Where would I rather be right now? What would I rather be doing? What's holding me back? Is fear whispering negative stuff in my ears? Am I too scared to make crucial decisions concerning my *Self*? Too busy to take a break?

You are probably tangled up in the issues of your life… regrets, discouragements, humiliations… and your approach in dealing with those issues might be the same as in the past; meaning you leave such matters to happenstance. Know that life will make decisions on your behalf, however, you must know that some of the decisions life will make for you might not be to your liking.

Your stuff needs your attention even if you are not able to sort out all of it immediately—stuff may take a while to complete. It is true, folks are attached to their natural personality and so they draw like-minded individuals to them (some might even believe zodiac signs could point them to the right attachments). For example, if you are too busy to choose and maintain meaningful relationships, before long you'll find yourself spending time in the company of 'friends' who are not heading your way. If you are convinced some of your stuff needs to be reorganized…do it now.

Love relationships, money, behavior (yours and others) are stuff that are really, really tricky and might even take precedence over *soul stuff*. So, if you are dealing with those kinds of stuff you may want to yield to *soul* stuff first *"Keep thy heart with all diligence; for out of it are the issues of life"* (*Proverbs 4:23*)

As you consider your stuff and the way you'd like to manage them, I ask you to also ponder the following true stories. You can raise a hand in affirmation if any of these accounts ring true—no one is watching. You might assert, after you've read an account, *this is the state of my life; this was the state of my life at one time; I will not let this be the state of my life any more.* Know that whatever you say stays in your heart and in your ears.

Isiah: Isiah was not really a bad person, he was just shifty. He worked on a farm, picking grapes, in Vineland. He was familiar with the punishment to farmworkers who go AWOL before their contract expiry, yet he contemplated the move. Isiah's problem was that he had little faith in himself. He didn't believe it was possible for him to fulfil his dream of graduating with a Bachelor's degree in social sciences... not unless he could contrive a scheme to have someone finance his university education. He found a Christian woman on a dating site who liked him enough to buy into his idea of leaving the farm and going to college. The relationship got off to a good start. The lady agreed to finance his education. He collected several thousand dollars from her, but instead of going off to college he initiated his getaway from the farm and secretly returned to his homeland. Isiah's behaviour left the woman in a deep financial hole. Clearly, Isiah never cared about obtaining higher education.

Folks target what they want and some will take from other people's resources without feelings of guilt or shame, which means all the same to them. I can tell you right now, when you are wishy-washy in any area of your life, people notice. For many, being wishy-washy in a situation might be better than turned away or snubbed. And the people who get taken advantage of, are folks who are perceived as unworthy—likely by those they love: spouse, children, close friends, and colleagues.

You might be blamed for being in a situation that causes you pain. You might be accused of not paying attention to the things you do, or even be ignored because you no longer matter. Know that what may be occurring in your difficult moment may be God's way of moving you to higher ground. It might be your moment to make a serious decision concerning your future plans. I'm not saying it will be easy because other people will continue their attempts to define you. Always think about your best interests and be mindful that other people are thinking about *their* own interests. Know that it is okay to be selfish about your interests.

Gordon: Gordon is forty-something, a successful IT professional and firstborn to a single teenaged mother named Marianne. He's married with two lovely children. Gordon never met his biological father. Word is, Gordon's father left Marianne on the day Gordon was born. Okay. Marianne obviously raised a good son for Gordon talks highly about his hardworking mother.

When Gordon was 35 years old, a man showed up claiming to be his father. Marianne confirmed the claim. That was not welcome news for Gordon. A reunion with his father raised emotions of anger, abandonment, resentment and hate. He did not want a get-together with a father who had deserted him more than thirty years. Marianne had obviously forgiven Gordon's father. She was a Christian woman and had raised good children under adverse circumstances. Children? Yes, children. Marianne has three more children. Like Gordon, Marianne's other children turned out well in the face of desertion by their respective fathers. I listened to Gordon's story without casting judgement. Life just is what it is. Here's the rub—Marianne (now in her sixties) had obviously been standing on unsound footing all those decades ago. She became comfortable where she stood— never recognising that she could move to a higher personal ground. The sad part about Marianne's situation is, she's still living vicariously through her children.

It is true, some parents raise loving, upstanding children in spite of challenges. The question is: At what point in an individual's life does the individual take personal responsibility for his or her falsehood and yield to his or her authentic *Self*? When is it okay to let go of crutches (spouse, children, relative, friends) and begin to do for *you*? What will your personal legacy be? Have you been living outside of your *Self* for so long that you're not even aware of the authentic you? Are most things about you unreal? Is there a victim persona within you, aiming at unsuspecting individuals— spouses, children, family and friends—to prop you up? It is time to carve out your path and begin a new way forward.

Barry and Ingrid: Barry and Ingrid lived together for three years. In the beginning they were in, what I call, a corporate love relationship. She, a well-paid company executive, didn't mind financing Barry while he finished law school. In time, they fell in love and the two of them became comfortable with each other. Barry had a habit of introducing Ingrid to friends and colleagues as his wife. Ingrid didn't agree with Barry because they were not yet married. Not that Ingrid hadn't been nudging Barry to make the relationship legal. Finally, Ingrid followed the advice of her best friend and gave Barry an ultimatum: "Marry me now or else…." Ingrid was certain her ultimatum would be immediately satisfied but that was not the case. Barry's reply to Ingrid's ultimatum stunned her "I've been meaning to tell you... ..." he said, and then he dropped a dirty bomb. All along, Barry had been hedging so that he could finish law school with Ingrid's support. Unfortunately, Ingrid had waited until she was up to her neck in sinking sand before she confronted Barry.

You know you are in a dead end love relationship when you're sharing closet space and toothpaste with someone for more than a year and you still don't know where the relationship is heading; when you've been engaged for more than a year and wedding bells have not started to ring; when your parents keep telling you its past time to make them grandparents; and when the fear of abandonment is whispering in your ear. I say, be authentic, especially to yourself. Tell yourself the truth about what you are feeling and take rectifying steps to be certain about where you stand. I also say be prepared to accept what you get if you stand back with folded arms waiting for a turn. Always remember, life will make decisions on your behalf and life's decisions might not be what you agree with. Don't accommodate a 'serious' relationship if fear of any kind is hanging over your head. If your relationship makes you feel sad, don't hesitate to take action that will make you feel better. Pay attention to what is happening in your domain.

Gemma and friends: Gemma is a beautiful woman. She is well read, and has always been independent. She is upfront about her relationships. She will tell you that she 'doesn't play' when it comes to love relationships. The moment Gemma finds out that things aren't working to her satisfaction she is ready to move on. The problem with Gemma is, her 'serious' relationships over the years, left footprints belonging to five children, the aftermath of each unsuccessful relationship.

Life will give folks more of what they seek until they're certain about what they truly desire. Some folks will return to the stuff (situations/relationships) they're comfortable with, even though they know it to be far better to learn a lesson as it is presented and make the next relationship a better one. I've always believed folks who keep doing what they're doing must like the results they're getting. Yes/No? So if folks don't like the results, I say make a change!

You are your experiences—good and not so good, decide what you don't want in order to attract what you want. Understand that developing patterns show themselves quickly. It is true some folks take a longer time to learn a lesson, other folks only need to drop to their knees once and they get it!

You may think you are doing all the right things to advance your circumstances and yet, you still find yourself in sticky mire. Ask yourself the following questions: What (who) is drawing me to this habit? What do I like about it? How does my ambition relate to this habit? What is hindering me from doing something different? What is the role of other people in all of this? People notice when you are in mire; they see your mistakes and they have a tendency to judge.

Always remember, past mistakes are just that; *past*. If your inclination is to keep looking back then understand that fear will keep you linked to your past in a wounded way. Banish fear. Move to higher ground. Leave the people who judge you behind—on their footing.

Moira and Canute: Ringing in the New Year with her Aunt Louise sounded like a good idea to Moira when she answered the long-distance ringtone and the invitation from her favorite aunt in New York to visit for a special New Year's event. Moira had just experienced a personal disappointment and her world had crashed.

The days following Christmas Day had been very challenging—a distraction would therefore be welcome.

"We'll go to watch night service and then enjoy my after dinner party," Aunt Louise told Moira as an enticement to get her to come to New York.

"Party after watch night service, Aunt Lou? I'm in… I'll be on the Greyhound bus tomorrow… meet me at the bus station in New York." Moira packed her little black dress and more essential pieces in her week-end bag for her trip.

"I'm in a gravel pit," Moira told her Aunt Lou when she enquired if Moira was bringing a male guest. Moira is a smart woman, at least she knew on what ground she stood at that moment.

Moira sensed her relationship with Canute was tentative. They had been dating for about nine months when he asked her if he could move in with her. She was reluctant to let him in but for several reasons: the weather was becoming chilly, he had been laid off from his job at the plastic bottle factory, he was three months behind in his rent, and, poor Canute, his landlord had given him notice to vacate. Fine. He was, as well, a Christian man. He had even encouraged Moira to come with him to his church. That was fine too. The clincher for Moira? Canute's dexterity as a lover was unsurpassed by anyone she'd known.

It was Christmas Eve. Christmas day was forecasted to be white. Moira felt at ease knowing she would be spending Christmas with a companion she liked.

Canute had left the apartment to attend to last minute holiday shopping. Moira relaxed and waited for him to return. Around 11 p.m., Canute called to say he was with his cousin Derrick having a drink. At 12 midnight, Canute called again, this time his speech was slurred. He told Moira he had had too much to drink and he would hang out at Derrick's until early Christmas morning. That was a wise decision Moira decided and then went to sleep. On Christmas morning, around seven o'clock, just before he boarded his flight to the Cameroons, Canute called Moira to say goodbye. In a letter to Moira, delivered by Derrick, Canute explained why he was never returning to her.

Moira was nobody's fool. She'd been listening keenly to Canute's conversations about his family back in his homeland (to be honest he never talked about a wife and children). But life in North America is good, so who would want to return to a homeland of poverty? But wait, Canute had never said he was poor in his homeland. Moira had a gut feeling that her relationship with Canute was uncertain. In a conversation with her best friend she revealed that Canute might not be the right man for her. Still she hoped she was wrong. When you know that you know, then go with what you know because you're usually right. It's your sixth sense at work.

We don't always understand why a relationship goes sour or a trust is broken. However, we are often our own best advisor; I say, listen to what you are intuitively telling yourself and act accordingly. You can make adjustments that will vindicate a bad experience, so you don't have to replay unwanted experiences. When Spirit is working through you, your life situations may look chaotic and weird. The Divine is pushing hard so that He can remove a stumbling block out of your way. For example, your marriage may be falling apart through no fault of your own; your children may be disrespecting you because you don't let them have their way; and your friends may be shunning you because you've fallen on hard times. Know that you're going through this course of surviving hell because God is about to remove a great stone out of your way. When it is time, nothing can stop you from receiving the favour that you were promised by your Heavenly Father and you will marvel when you exit from the mire that bogs you down. I know this because I've had experiences that floored me for my own good. When you find yourself in a moment of disappointment you should stand still and assess where you are and where you think you want to be. Then, ask to be guided to higher ground. Higher ground is where folks get a better view and a new perspective.

Pastor Gerald and Daphne: Daphne rented the top floor of her city duplex to Gerald, the new pastor. Gerald had just set up church in a vacant unit at the neighbourhood mall, the residents in the area were already starved for the Word from a spiritual leader; as a result, his ministry was welcome.

Very quickly, Gerald became an admired pastor. Word circulated about his gift of healing; financial donations from the congregation multiplied. But Gerald was a womanizer—always been and that was the reason he found himself in that part of the city, a place where he thought his past indiscretions would not catch up to him. Gerald developed a fleshly relationship with Daphne. Daphne was sure she would become Gerald's wife. Life was good until that fateful Sunday morning when Gerald's lawful wife showed up in church. When she announced her identity, the congregation was stunned. Gerald was sure his heart would attack him! He recognized he was standing in sinking sand. He had to think fast—his sermon that Sunday morning was short and to the point:

This woman is trying to damage my name, ruin my reputation, and bring the church down. Know this, whatever she says about me is all lies, lies I say. I am your God-sent shepherd and I will lead you on a right and proper path. And blah, blah, blah.

Mia and Basil: Mia, Basil's girlfriend, told friends how much she admired Basil's motivation. He had been *taking* self-improvement courses in college—quick, short courses in computers, travel, and customer service—to find a 'decent' paying job. Mia had been minding the home front—only until such time as Basil completed his latest course. When Mia inquired of Basil how soon he might find a job he told her he had no plans to look for a job. In fact, all along Basil had been maintaining an improper relationship. Mia let him go!

Ezra and Jasmine: Ezra had been chums with Jasmine during high school. They're now adults and they live in different cities. Ezra is married with family. By chance, Ezra reconnected with Jasmine while on vacation. The connection took root. He welcomed the distraction because the home front had broken down and he was awaiting final divorce papers. Things happened really fast between Jasmine and Ezra; they wanted to be together. So, Jasmine planned a destination wedding. They became man and wife. Sounds pretty decent—right? Didn't take long for Jasmine to discover that Ezra wasn't manager at a large corporation like he said, nor was he earning a five-digit salary each month—an outright fib. Furthermore, he had to give up his portion of the proceeds from the sale of his beautiful home in the suburbs of Toronto as part of the divorce settlement, and his company re-claimed the high-end SUV he had been driving. In addition, the daily calls from Ezra's creditors were becoming overwhelming for Jasmine. Ezra could not put *humpty dumpty together again*. Two deceptive people. Yes, Jasmine was also a deceiver because when she reconnected with Ezra she had just exited a ten-year relationship that left her distraught and she was determined to prove to her former partner that she was still relevant—Ezra was Jasmine's rebound.

Zipurah Beckford: Zipurah Beckford's husband, Michael, was in the international entertainment business. He travelled long distances quite often and when he was not in transit, he was coordinating business transactions with clients on his cell phone. Purah, as Zipurah is affectionately called, never meddled in Michael's business although she had a sinking feeling some things smelled *fishy* when she overheard some of his phone conversations.

Zipurah's story goes like this: It was a warm August evening. She was hustling home from her part-time job at the bank to prepare dinner for her family. She was walking briskly when Michael's Chevy van pulled up alongside her. "Hop in, honey," Michael said.

"I wanted to be home before you, Mike," Zipurah laughed and hopped into the passenger side of the Chevy van. "You are home early this evening—how come?"

"Cedrick is visiting us later; he's carrying a parcel from Winnie—haven't seen Cedrick since he left for Toronto three years ago. We'll have a drink or two and talk about old times," Michael answered.

"Oh yes—I remember—Cedrick is here on vacation—and he is spending only one night with us?" Zipurah asked.

"He has business to take care of in the city," Michael replied.

Michael and Zipurah greeted their two children, Shernette 6 and Darnell 3, at the gate of their modest three-bedroom bungalow, located on Bell Street.

"Ma—Cedrick is coming here tonight—you remember Cedrick, your favourite son-in-law," Michael told his mother. Mother Morgan pouted, "I remember him alright—how can I forget him, he took my baby girl from me and married her... and he still has not given up his crooked ways."

"Winnie is not a baby, Ma," Michael said and kissed his Mother on the head. "And Cedrick is not as crooked as you think," he continued. With all hands on deck dinner was ready well before Cedrick's arrival.

"Come in Bro," Michael greeted Cedrick when he appeared at the door.

"A long time," Cedrick said hugging Michael and slapping him on the back.

Mother Morgan appeared at the kitchen door, "Howdy, Cedrick, how come you left my baby girl in Toronto?"

"Mother Morgan, can't you at least ask me how I've been doing? Your baby girl in Toronto is just fine," Cedrick laughed and kissed Mother Morgan on the cheek.

Zipurah waited for her turn to greet Cedrick—not exactly her favourite brother-in-law. He'd been involved in several "scrapes" and his slate was by no means clean.

"How are your two boys—they must be grown up now," Zipurah chimed.

"Sixteen and nineteen," Cedrick answered.

"Dinner is ready," Mother Morgan called out to Shernette and Darnel who had been playing on the verandah. The family sat down to dinner. Later, Zipurah yawned and stretched, it was well past her bedtime. "Goodnight, Mike," she said to Michael.

"See you in the morning, Purah," Michael replied.

"Good night, Ma," Michael said.

Good night all," Cedrick said.

Zipurah went to sleep with her two children tightly tucked-in at her side.

It was around 2.00 in the morning when Zipurah awoke to a medley of Bob Marley's songs playing on the turntable in her living room. Michael and Cedrick were talking and laughing and the neighbourhood dogs were barking. It sounded like the dogs converged at her front gate although it was not unusual for all the dogs to bark at the same time, especially early mornings. The sound of vehicles driving along Bell Street added to the noise. Zipurah was finding it difficult to go back to sleep.

"Those dogs bark nonstop at night," Zipurah heard Michael telling Cedrick. Then she heard a thud against the side of the house. She peered into the living room and saw Michael walking over to the open grilled window. He parted the drapery to look.

Pow!

The loud pop, sounded like a fire cracker. Michael fell back against the wall. Then she heard Cedrick hollering, "Mike get shot. Mike get shot."

Michael was lying face down on the living room floor, when the police and ambulance arrived. He was pronounced dead minutes later at the hospital.

In the aftermath, all kinds of speculation crossed Zipurah's mind. What was the true intention of the gunman? Was he a lone gunman or were there others with him? Was the incident an attempted robbery? Was it a twist of fate that Cedrick was visiting when the murder occurred? Those questions bothered Zipurah for many months. She was angry. Fear of the unknown possessed her. "I feel like I'm standing on a pile of shifting rocks," Zipurah told her Pastor.

Zipurah ran away from supposed hit men in her homeland and put herself at the mercy of the country of refuge. Zipurah was a smart woman for though the rocks beneath her feet shifted, she found her way to solid ground, meaning she found a way to live a peaceful life in spite of her unpleasant memories. (Exiled in Canada).

This is the truth: You might be 'enjoying' a life that looks good to an observer and yet the life doesn't *feel good* to you. You're thinking fear must be raising its ugly head. You sit precariously on the edge of your situation because you know hell has to *break loose* and release the tension. You *throw* caution to the wind—that is not good. Have a conversation with *Self*... ask *Self* some pointed questions and surrender to the answers. Remember, you are your best advisor.

Deceit/Lying/Tricks

Truth is what we express with confidence and conviction even though others folks may disagree, truth is our response to truth from others, truth is word and action on one accord.
—Great is Thy Faithfulness, *Olive Rose Steele*

Some people believe deceit, lying, and tricks are simple dishonesties to be glossed over and should be amicably handled between partners, friends and family—in other words, *it is a funny thing—just a joke* In such instances, the deceivers and cheaters are having their cake and eating it too and that should not be accepted.

If some things seem too good to be true, you know that a lie is in the midst. Some people don't realize that their untruth adversely affects other people. Lies are bad. People lose integrity when they're found to be lying. Lies should never be taken for jokes. Call it untruth, fib, falsehood, myth—it is still a lie.

Fear tells folks to lie as a way of protecting *Self.* Then fear turns to anger because that is fear's way of seeming credible. Forgive you for not telling the truth and forgive everyone that participated in the lie. It is better to be upfront than to be shamed by a lie.

For example: Dana learned through the 'grapevine' about Johnson's infidelity. She courageously ended their relationship. The end was more chaotic than she imagined—family and friends made it their business to be involved in the final say—Dana and Johnson never thought the end of their relationship would impact the lives of other people in such an unpleasant way. Their emotions went from love to hurt to resentment to sadness. Pity.

Hurt will hang around longer if folks dwell on it. I have said, when you find yourself in a sticky love relationship mire admit responsibility sooner rather than later; take a positive position; forgive the individuals involved (including yourself) and then make a dignified exit.

Every contrary situation cries out for a reunion (now or later). Yield to your inner strength (Spirit within). Reunite with your transgressors to ease your mind. The rest is God's business.

What (or who) is your rock?

In a practical way, you and I have a good idea of what rocks are. Rocks lie on the ground everywhere; we can't help but notice them. We toss them around, stand on them, lean on them, sit on them, and we form them into backdrops. The word rock is often used to describe a gem stone, a heavy-metal band, a relationship, a place of worship. And quite often folks have described a *rock* as shaky (rock the boat).

Your rock might be a spouse, your family, children, an occupation, a business, an education, faith and belief, the return to a certain place and even a walking stick. So I ask you: What (or who) is your rock? You might say this is a trick question though you will admit you could point to something, someone or somewhere as your rock. It might not be easy to define another person's rock (need, dependency, comfort zone, reliance, and support). For example, you might be a 'nice' person however, if someone messes with your rock you could go berserk.

My rock is the principle upon which I stand; my belief; the tower of my strength which is Spirit within; my strong post, my steady course, my safe zone. My rock is about my doing; it is the markers I leave on the sands of time, to be seen and understood by those who will walk on those sands.

I have said deception is a dirty trick. For example, if you trusted in your rock and got let down, you might feel hurt for a long time, even if you had cut your losses and swore never to trust again—it usually happens—again. Every person will accept that they might be duped at least once. I set my dupe limit at four; meaning I will only allow myself to be deceived four times and then I'll step on my brakes and say; *no more.* My cousin, Thelma keeps adding to her dupe limit; she was at six when we last spoke, that's because she's been giving herself more chances to be duped. All I'm saying is; don't allow yourself to be fooled too many times. Remember deceit is ugly and upsetting; deceit undermines friendships and relationships, and results in loss of integrity; deceit is fear raising its ugly head. When you encounter dishonesty move to a rock that is higher.

Your Rock and your Stuff

Stuff you label as your Rock is what you're not ready to part with. Your rock and your stuff are true allies. At the beginning of this Section, I identified some tangible stuff that might make your life run smoothly. However, your stuff could arouse jealousy in other folks. The stuff you own could be envied by folks who feel they have to *take you down* to get what you have. Why? Because it is much easier for them to take your stuff than to work hard to acquire their own stuff.

You've been firm in protecting your stuff. You put up barriers and set boundaries. Still, folks act inappropriately to take away your stuff—that's how it is sometimes. I say, forgive other people's inappropriate behaviour and pray for them to overcome their fear of lack.

Self

Self, is the divine part of you and I. *Self* might be symbolised by a personal connection with Divine Spirit (God). It is that part of us that says "I am". The phrase "I am" should always be followed by: good, happy, healthy, loving and whole. *Self* as the "I am" that should be explored.

Self is your true nature, your character, your Higher Spirit. Self seeks to replace Ego with love; Self will not accommodate other people's inconsiderate judgements. Self is the love side of your Ego Be merciful to your Self.
—Great is Thy Faithfulness, *Olive Rose Steele*

Some folks recognize *Self* as Me, Myself and I in a positive way. Others treat *Self* like an annoying addendum to their big ego. Whereas Self is loving, giving, happy, healthy, and whole, ego, the flippant side of *Self*, expresses fear in many forms. *Self* displays right feelings; triggers right words, and directs and guides folks toward right actions.

Self is your best ally, the love side of your ego. *Self* continuously upholds its loving, well-adjusted nature for our benefit. Even with its clear distinction and actions *Self* could be misinterpreted as solely about *who* folks believe they are—unless, of course, folks are rooted in good principles.

Self deserves to be cared for. I'm not talking about fed, clothed, and sheltered for that is assumed, I am referring to care that nurtures the soul. I cannot say enough about the need to be conscious of *Self*. Folks who recognize *Self* as the all-important nature of humankind recognize undesirable egos that show up in subtle ways. I've always said *Self* is your true nature, your character, and *Self* will not accommodate inconsiderate judgements. In your quiet moments with *Self* you learn a lot about the true you. Yield to your *Self*-ish moments; be thankful for the part of your nature that is your *Self*.

Surrender. Trust your *Self* to bring all of your needs in alignment with your true nature, for your good. You are equipped to handle the issues of your life. Allow *Self* to be guided by your *Built-in Prayer Mechanism* as it prompts you to pray and trust Spirit to make your outcomes positive. (The term; *Built-in Prayer Mechanism* is explained in my book; Great is Thy Faithfulness).

Steadfast reliance on your *Built-in Prayer Mechanism* and its connection to your *Self*, will activate Divine power within and lift your faith to a higher level at the right moment.

Self / Ego / Fear

You recognize and understand your ego's desire to get your attention and since ego's agenda is to divide and conquer, *Self* has to be on guard when ego appears in its different forms and masks to deceive. Some folks might be cautious about parsing *Self* and ego. But I say, it is a good thing to analyse the two for in doing so, folks can be acquainted with the virtue of *Self* and the rascal of ego. Don't be deceived, ego will come at you through other people; guard your *Self* against other people's ego when it (ego) shows up as fear. Know that everything you thought to be negative about your *Self* is untrue. And everything negative that other people say about your *Self* is also untrue.

I caution folks that fear will attack from all angles. For example, when you find yourself tilting toward indecisions you should know that ego is at work in the form of fear. Consider life after a fear attack. Did fear floor you? Did you banish fear? Is what you're seeing through your mind's eye pleasing? Is your ego tamed to the point where *Self* is in control? Know that a decision to make needed changes has placed you on a divine path.

From time to time, the egos and fears of other people, have challenged folks as *other people's business* and that is why I say, be cautious about getting into other people's business because other people's business could use up your energy and wear you down. Folks need to identify fear when it shows up as other people's business and deal with it appropriately. I'll say it again, fear makes its approach using various disguises and forms. As a result, no matter how it shows up, what form it takes and how huge it is, you are not oblige to fight other people's fear-based battles. Take care of your own business (fears). Ego should be kept under wraps.

In my book *Great is thy Faithfulness* I talk about *Ego* as follows:

Ego is all about itself: me, myself, and I; Ego is insecure, it is in love with itself only, it demands admiration and keeps true Self fearful so that true Self will come back for stimulus; Ego is a companion for life, it never gives up on its mission to control true Self; Ego's desire is to divide and conquer to maintain its influence over true Self; Ego promotes itself as true because it believes it is our true personality, our true character; the truth is, we develop and expand our Ego as we grow and mature in our environments; Ego sees a motionless position as passive and it encourages us to show we are in charge; Ego insists that we hold our stance and pushes us to take what is ours if we felt we were deceived; Ego will appear in different ways, wearing different masks, to distract us; Ego constantly reminds us of our importance and it will appear in every form imaginable to jog our memory about who we believe we are; this is our Ego's way of maintaining self-interest; ego is arrogant, it makes us take notice of our status and some of us exert our privilege standing by squashing and dishonouring the status and talents of other people; Ego lets us believe we are the sum total of our lineage, our beliefs, our achievements, and our possessions.

Are you in a battle—a battle in which ego tells you one thing and *Self* tells you another thing? Are you in a battle to end an unhealthy bond? Are you in a battle for perfect health, a custody battle; a battle over finances, a battle with a child who wants to come back home; or perhaps a child who needs to become independent? Are you trying to make something of a negative situation? Whatever the battle, everyone wants victory or a firmer stance. Know that if you find yourself on unfavourable ground you can begin the journey to a better place.

Where you are, you're not alone—Spirit within is with you, directing and guiding you at all times. You don't need to stay in uncomfortable places because of fear. You *can do* what you want to do; you *can be* what you choose to be!

Throughout this book I persistently *take on* ego and fear. I do so because I recognize my attachment to the two of them. I am aware of the games ego play and so I struggle to be more of *Self*. Through my experiences, the only fear I now cling to is the Fear of God.

Fear or nightmare?

Folks often refer to some of their fears as their worst nightmares. And it becomes tricky if other people's fears get into the mix. Other people's fears will weave in and out of your life without your permission and in subtle ways that will leave you fretful. And it is not because folks are ignorant of the effect of other people's fear, it is likely because they're not ready to stand up and face fear when it raises its ugly head. Fear is a deceiver. Fear will show up in your life in different forms to trick you. I say, banish fear and permit *Self*, to thrive in a spiritual atmosphere.

I determine that fear will hinder folks from making important decisions and even necessary changes. For example, you discover your spouse's pornography habit and you know you should address the situation, but your spouse is heavy-handed and controlling; your grown children's aggressive behaviour in your home is becoming intolerable, it's time for them to be on their own; you know the situation calls for disciplining, but your fear of loss of love kicks in and holds you back from addressing the issue; your best friend's betrayal floors you, you know you should speak up about her disloyalty, but fear of abandonment intervenes and causes you to hold back. The foregoing situations are nightmarish and require decisive actions but folks might be mired in fear.

On the other hand, some folks talk about their *worst nightmare*, like it is a necessary evil; they remain absorbed with the issues of their life. When fear suggests chaos is in the cards, conflict is on the horizon and pain is expected, I say fear not! No matter what it is, it has no *teeth* unless it bites.

Dear God
I am challenged by fear in its different guises
Threatened by fear from all sides
I cannot fight these terrible fears
They hinder my logical thinking
And my ability to make right decisions
Help me to know only the fear of
God, give me courage to stand my
ground, let me trust in You alone
Hold my hand through this difficulty
And give me Your peace
—*Olive Rose Steele*

Change

Change may occur at any point in your life and some of those changes might not be under your control. Changes such as illness, bereavement, separation, divorce, and loss of income can throw you in a tizzy. Whether you decide your own change or life initiates it for you, it is wise to roll with the punches in that moment, as you move to a higher ground.

Tell your Ego to settle down and be quiet so that you can attend to *Self.* You may need to change a thought pattern, change an unhealthy relationship, a job, an address or a lifestyle. You may even have to cut some folks loose, still it doesn't have to be a radical change.

Change can be tricky when you try to help other people in their struggle to change. Not everyone will be ready to

51

accept your support. They may not take your advice. Don't be hard on them. They will change when they receive a *hotter clap*. It is much easier to show the change you would like other people to make by your example.

My favourite catchphrase is: *Eyes are always watching*. Be the change others notice. You might be surprised to learn there are people who would like to emulate your life. Your change could impact the lives of more people than you care to even acknowledge. It's the kind of change you accept as *beyond your control*.

Your change cannot remain a secret, for networks will do what networks do best—serve as megaphones to broadcast what they know. Your change may simplify or complicate your life; you decide how you manage your change. The change you make could replace, replicate, and multiply. Be authentic.

Observe your fear masks. What are you covering up? Know that when you have too much stuff under a lid you are disempowering *Your Self*.

You might be hurting from a failed or broken past relationship, take heart, all is not lost for negative experiences can have positive outcomes. Folks before you have survived the onslaught of negative experiences and live to talk about them—it's all in your point-of-view. You don't need to develop a set behaviour pattern to handle difficulties. Try not to acknowledge or value dysfunctional situations; identify them quickly and deal with them for if you don't, they will deplete your energy and cause nagging headaches. Don't wait around for bad situations to change by themselves, move to a higher ground! It is never too late to make changes for your good. Make the change.

In this Part 2, we explore a *salad bar* loaded with stuff that I believe will create a balanced platter. As we go into Part 3, you will notice more of the same fixings, dressed up slightly different. Enjoy the menu. Have bite size pieces—for now.

Are you in a battle—a battle in which ego tells you one thing and *Self* tells you another thing? Are you in a battle to end an unhealthy bond? Are you in a battle for perfect health, a custody battle; a battle over finances, a battle with a child who wants to come back home; or perhaps a child who needs to become independent? Are you trying to make something of a negative situation? Whatever the battle, everyone wants victory or a firmer stance. Know that if you find yourself on unfavourable ground you can begin the journey to a better place.

PART THREE

Our Stuff

Let me tell you what I mean when I mention 'stuff.' Stuff is physical and metaphysical; it is the mental clutter in our heads and the physical clutter around us; it is relationships, good and bad; it is negativity, ours and others'; it is bad attitude, ours and others'; it is prejudice born of hurt, malice or belief system; it is 'baggage' from our past that we lug around in life. All of us carry similar yet unique 'stuff'.

—Olive Rose Steele

THE *STUFF* WE talked about in Sections 1 and 2 as *My Stuff* and *Your Stuff* now becomes *Our Stuff*. Our *stuff* is unavoidably tied up with other people's stuff. The term *Our Stuff* signifies that other folks are in the picture. Therefore, it is not easy to set *My Stuff* and *Your Stuff* apart from *Our Stuff* for the reason that stuff is generally the same when they are wrapped up. I will say this, if you mind your own business, *Your Stuff* (good and bad) will be your stuff, no matter what.

You might be one of the fortunate people who've done everything the right way. You show respect for others as required; you're educated; you hold down a nice job and you have a loving family. Yet you feel like you're standing at a thorny uncomfortable place. You know that if you stay there, you will choke for that is not where you want to be standing.

But let us assume you are at your perfect place; you are happy, healthy and whole; you are rejoicing and the LOVE word is easy for you to say. Folks who recognise you seem happy for you, and yet, they're amazed that you're still standing, as far as they know, you should be wobbling. Then, without any action on your part, a stranger enters your domain. You're not sure you want to be friendly or even be side-tracked. What now? Read on.

Our Stuff could make us legally responsible for what is happening in other people's domain. For example marriage, family, children, business, and people whom you probably will never meet could impact your *world* in a negative and/or positive way. And because some of *Our stuff* is universally tangled up—spiritual, financial, health issues, world events and much more—we ought to make it our business to be aware of how other people's stuff stacks on to *Our Stuff*. I say pay close attention to what is going on!

We were not meant to survive without other people, yet many of us will confine ourselves to our own *world* for conveniences and peace of mind. Basically our *world* consists of our spouse, family, friends, colleagues and people we allow to come in and stay for however long we let them. We can make our *world* as large or as small as we desire.

Whether we like it or not, our *world* is active, things happen which involve us and require our attention 24/7. And folks mitigate the impact of things that happen in their *world* by setting up protective barriers—I call these barriers lines of demarcation. Marriages, love relationships, agreements, deals, higher learning, professions, associations, church affiliations, and places of abode are just some barriers people use to keep other people from entering their domain.

All the same, folks should recognize that barriers create preconceptions. All should acknowledge that we live shared lives, however, when we find our self at a place where what might be happening has nothing to do with us I say, make a hasty dash to higher ground?

The following stories are real. As always, names have been changed to protect their privacy. Please read with an open mind.

Donna, Michael and Jerome

Donna: Donna's father physically abused her mother because that's what his father before him had done. Donna's grandfather told her father that such an action kept Donna's grandmother (and his other women) submissive and dutiful. Donna's father eventually made an effort to stop doing the bad things he knew his father had done to his mother. He realizes his daughter, Donna, could marry a man who treats her just as badly as he treated her mother. Donna's father put a stop to the generational domestic abuse pattern.

Michael: Michael was described as a *good kid*. This good kid took a wrong turn with a bad crowd and began drug dealing. Michael defended his bad habit by claiming his choice of *work* was his only means of making good money. Michael was locked up for six years, enough time for him to come to the realization that drug dealing should not be considered a career.

Jerome: No one wants to be around an angry person, let alone sharing living spaces with one and yet sometimes folks do. Anger is a bad attitude and someone with a bad attitude always finds something to be angry about.

Jerome verbally and physically abuses Kathy. She cries. He apologizes. They make up. They do this routinely. Kathy reasons she might be responsible for Jerome's anger issues, *she* changes some things about herself. Jerome recognizes Kathy's submission to his bad behavior and finds more things to be angry about. Kathy is brave, she warns Jerome she would leave him unless he seeks anger management counseling. Jerome didn't. Kathy left Jerome.

Other people (spouse, children family, and friends) will use our good and not so good stuff to their advantage… it's how *Our Stuff* gets tangled up with other people's stuff. I say, look carefully into the stuff other people show you before you get tangled up with it. When you recognize that other people's stuff isn't good for you and you identify dysfunction, don't try to *work with it.* You may garnish a situation, hold your nose and live with a condition or you may even attempt to make modifications to spruce the stuff up, in the end you may just have to let it go and look after your business!

Aha, got some things that I want you to know now.
Just as sure as the winds gonna blow now
My Mommy told me, you better shop around
—Shop Around, *Written by Smokey Robinson and Barry Gordy*

Look closely, the other people's stuff is really their business and if you aren't watchful their stuff could mingle with *Your Stuff* and cause big complications.

What is standing in the way?

Fear. Fear disguised as distrust, envy, anger, resentment; those things we talked about before as *My Stuff* and *Your Stuff*. Some of *Our Stuff* might be genetic; some might be learned and some might be borrowed, all the bad stuff should be rejected. I say cast them off and go free.

Someone recently said to me: *Olive, you talk about fear as a negative emotion; I see fear differently … I embrace fear as a fact of life; a defensive mechanism; I use fear to protect myself.* Without question, I said. It is true, out of fear folks will retreat in fright (a house on fire; exploding firearms) but folks cannot run away from fear which is rooted in the thoughts.

Fear is a thief. If we let it, fear will come into our thoughts and rob us of our ability to function in a logical manner.

Fear will pop up in people's life as uncertainties, feelings of lack, injustice, disrespect, and hate. And folks must be ready to deal with fear when fear comes.

Hate, for example, is fear wanting to be loved—love turned inside out. Hate should be banished into nothingness where it belongs before it morphs into distrust. Distrust is fear's loss of credibility, it is a cruel trick; it makes people angry for no good reason. Anger is fear's inability to communicate a point of view clearly; fear makes people angry when they think everything else they have tried has failed. Anger can be managed if people take a moment to understand what brought on the anger. Fear becomes resentful when it believes it is being disrespected. Folks should know that respect attracts respect.

It is not unusual for folks to unintentionally put up with fear's devious, underhanded practices. For example, someone or something could slip into our domain under one of fear's false pretenses and cause havoc. Folks may even cause their own fear-based chaos but before folks beat up on themselves, they should pay attention to someone they know who has survived a similar mess. Do not surrender to fear that manifests itself in the form of a so called 'mess.' Make your world a fearless place; a place where courage reigns; a place filled with love. The people who are part of *our stuff* are there for a reason and likely for a season. And when it is time, they exit without a fuss.

How Stuff appears

Always look beyond appearances. Many will come to you claiming to be the one you asked for but only one will be authentic.
—I am the Door, *Paul Ferrini*

Stuff might not turn out the same if folks are not on the same wave length—meaning ultimate outcomes might not be for the wellbeing of everyone involved.

Dear God
This situation makes me feel helpless
I release my opinions; I relinquish my ideas
I lay down my human will; I put aside my human planning
I give up my ambitions; I abandon my pride and vanity
I now give this heavy burden to you
Father, I ask you to adjust and govern this situation
Take full control of the outcome and bless everyone involved
Amen
—*Olive Rose Steele*

When I pray: *Take full control of the outcome, and bless everyone involved*, I am acknowledging that I can do nothing to make the situation better. I am relinquishing the circumstances to a Higher Power to bring the outcome to a satisfactory conclusion for all concerned. I am giving up control knowing that all I need to do is ask God to make the situation right. I put aside doubt and I am waiting for an appropriate resolution. Let me tell you about Glenn and Sheila.

Glenn and Sheila: Glenn told Sheila he was married. That was an honest start to their relationship. Sheila, a *young senior* (I have no idea where I got that term from), is an independent divorcee. She owns a home and has her own tangible *stuff*. She spends many hours in her home studio, where she paints. The friendship which developed between Glenn and Sheila suited both their purposes. Glenn, an inactive real estate broker, knows it is time to let go of his real estate business and retire. He constantly complains about the state of affairs concerning his marriage and his pending divorce: his wife was driving a hard bargain, he said; she's asking for more than she deserves—half of everything including his pension, his life insurance policies and holdings. His wife is 'wicked', he told Sheila; and he can't wait for his divorce to be settled. Months add up. Glenn is sharing closet space and toothpaste with Sheila at her place and, *sometime*s, he uses his own toothpaste at his home. Okay. Glenn's divorce finally settled. His matrimonial home and chattels sold and divvied up between him, his wife and their three children. His share was not great. He'll survive. Sheila agreed to sell her place. They purchased a joint residence. Fine. Glenn became her husband, what could go wrong?

Did I tell you Sheila was an independent woman? Okay. She soon discovered that Glenn was, in her words, controlling and regularly angry for no apparent reason. Stuff which Sheila did not like, came into their home in the form of unannounced weekend and Sunday visits from Glenn's offspring. Glenn and Sheila's marriage was not going well. It appeared like Glenn and Sheila brought their stuff together in a negative way. Glenn's stuff was his denial about the reasons his first marriage broke up and Sheila's stuff was her inability to give and take with respect to Glenn's apparent lack of self-confidence.

Sometimes you pick up something, thinking it's something else, and by the time you realize what it really is, you got a real mess to clean up.
—Yesterday, I Cried, *Iyanla Vanzant.*

I admit, folks come into relationships with their own stuff. Most don't pay close attention to the stuff they bring with them. They reason: *what could be wrong with my stuff?* Yet, they look critically at the other person's stuff. Yes, it is good to give and take. But situations become lopsided when one gives more than one takes. Resentment will follow if there is no middle ground. When you know where you stand and you are honest and upfront in your dealings with the other folks, you can say 'yes' because you're sure, and you can say 'no' because you mean it. What you say matters.

Pay attention; crappy stuff and the carriers of such stuff might weave into your *world* when you aren't watching. It is messy and time consuming to clean up or fix other people's crappy stuff. Is crappy stuff fear? Yes, fear of abandonment, fear of loss of love, fear of being left behind—you name the fear; if it sneaks up on you, it is crappy.

We've looked at stuff from different viewpoints and we recognized that *Our Stuff* will intermingle with other people's stuff should we allow it. Some people will accept an amount of normal inconveniences in their dealings; however other people might pull back from having to be bothered at all.

In this Part 3, we examine *Our Stuff* as it relates to other people's business and true *Self* is the ultimate winner.

Our *stuff* could make us legally responsible for what is happening in other people's domain. For example marriage, family, children, business, and people whom you probably will never meet could impact your *world* in a negative and/or positive way.

***

Is crappy stuff fear? Yes, fear of abandonment, fear of loss of love, fear of being left behind—you name the fear; if it sneaks up on you, it is crappy.

PART FOUR

Belief, Spirituality, Self-help

The desire to savour life is, I believe, what drives many of us to the self-help isle in the first place. Most of us are not suffering a real addiction, not crippled by low-self-esteem, not battling repressed memories: These are the red herring of the self-help movement. What really drives us to seek help is an equally frightening sensation: that of being alive, yet not really living.

The Last Self-help Book You'll Ever Need
—*Dr. Paul Pearsall.*

TWO YEARS AGO I read a book titled: *The Last Self-Help Book You'll Ever Need* by Dr. Paul Pearsall, a bestselling author. In this book, Dr. Pearsall has written some alternatives to "selfhelpism" and the one nugget that stuck with me is his advice to readers to: "Delude Yourself" (as opposed to *do not* delude yourself). I have to say, it sounded outlandish. So I carefully considered Dr. Pearsall's advice and concluded that delusions (made-up impressions) might be just as helpful to some folks, in order to survive some of life's crucial moments. Why am I saying this? I've been called to give over my thoughts in written words. And the words I write emanate from a place within me—a place that is effervescent. Is this the Divine Spirit at work, a special gift, an ancestral knowing or just words that need to be expressed? Have I been deluding myself? Absolutely not. I have written facts in *The Solid Rock* that may have given you food for thought. If some of what I have written sounds odd—it may be that my personal experiences and my moments of truth do not occur at the same time as yours. It is true, folks don't have the same positive and negative feelings at the same time; however many can relay experiences which influence their lives in helpful and not so helpful ways. I say, observe crucial situations, make real decisions and snap back to reality as quickly as possible. Unlike Pearsall, I truly believe delusions should be fleeting.

Belief

Belief might be a point-of-view, an opinion; a conviction; confidence in thoughts and words as a fundamental part of one's life journey; an assurance that one can be the best at one's mission and an essential support system. Some people's belief stems from traditions, cultures, religions, rituals, and the news of the day. It is not uncommon for one's belief to disappoint when it turns out different from what one expected. People *lose faith* if the medical report had assured their healing and afterwards the illness returned; if the job interview did not go their way or their love relationship did not work out well. Is belief discriminatory? Did your belief let you down? Is it better to be conventional in your belief? Understand that your belief may emphasize your faith or challenge your basic assumptions, that's the "Is-ness" of life.

People, whose belief is dogmatic, are inclined to reach out to someone whom they perceive as devout who has the ability to meet their need for further spiritual outreach. For example, a Priest, a Pastor, an Imam, perhaps a Guru, someone to shepherd them through their thoughts—a *smorgasbord* for their spiritual appetite. Folks who reach out in such circumstances might run into deceitful guides, consequently many rely on Christian media as a modern day replacement for brick and mortar church buildings.

Christian Media

Public broadcasting is a convenient conduit for religious teachings and Christian media is a fact of today's living. Observe the intense merchandising that accompanies TV church; listen to unrestricted requests for large monetary contributions, the sale of CDs, DVDs, books, fees for mega conferences in huge auditoriums. These resources are marketed under the banner of taking the Gospel to the world at large. It is true that successful preaching feed beliefs through media marketing. And please don't misunderstand me for I believe all should be awakened to truth.

But folks should acknowledge religious marketing as big business and business enterprises are not always reliable. I believe it is wise for folks to identify advertising repetitions occurring on different platforms, and only take what is needed from what is given.

Someone asked me recently; what is my belief—do I *know God?* The question was asked in a manner that made me wonder if she thought I *did not know* God. To be respectful I answered that I do *know* God planted me on this earth for a specific purpose; I am aware of God's absolute power; I *know* that God provided me with everything I needed to survive this life; and when I look around I see God's love demonstrated in creation.

But seriously, what qualifies someone to ask another such a question? Pompous religious beliefs will give the impression that only creeds that are related to certain churches are right and proper. I'm not certain whether my reply was suitable for my questioner; however, I rest on my core belief, which is in God and His goodness.

Since places of worship offer religious teachings and opinions; people will try the ones that they like and they will go to the church of their choosing. The fact is, seeing is believing, therefore, folks have an opportunity to witness beliefs in action—live and through media.

I met Sonia, a Christian woman, during a transit jaunt. When we introduced ourselves we discovered we were from the same neighbourhood and, we were familiar with some of the same people and places. Sonia invited me to her place of worship. I attended. Sonia says her Pastor is a good person; he loves Jesus, prays for miracles, and exhorts his flocks to give ten percent of their earnings (and even more) to assist in spreading the Gospel. Sounds like a good shepherd? Yes? Sonia confided she was not happy with Pastor's decision to purchase the half-an-hour time slot on TV to spread the Gospel. And she laughed nervously when she talked about her purchase of a large filing cabinet to keep the religious books, DVDs and CDs she'd purchased. In addition, Pastor's private *stuff* included two beautiful homes, a luxury car, and enough toys to keep him and his family happy. Fine. It is what it is. Sonia's pastor is blessed. The problem I have with a scenario such as this is; Sonia and most (if not all) of the members of the congregation aren't as blessed as Pastor. Why not?

It is not unusual for onlookers to question other people's extravagances (stuff), especially when their own situations are dismal.

Good people are priests, pastors, teachers, doctors, prominent community individuals, etc.; and these good people can be selfish. Quite often good people make bold-faced personal (self-serving) decisions in the name of their fundamental beliefs. Please forgive me if I'm wrong, but I believe blatant selfish decisions should be unacceptable. Being a good person has little to do with religious beliefs. It has everything to do with charitable giving.

Dear God,
Use me to bring comfort to others
Use the words I speak
Use my expressed feelings
Use my actions towards others to draw them to you
Let me say words that others need to hear
Let me do things that need to be done
Let your beauty be seen in me
And let everything I do be done to the honor
and glory of Your Name
—Olive Rose Steele

Authenticity

Religious and non-religious folks often second guess their right/wrong track. They're not certain if they are living up to perfect standards. It seems to them like something is not altogether real in some areas of their life; be it at home, at work, at play, in finances, with health and in their belief. I venture to say, right now, nothing is wrong. Really? Yes, everything is as it should be. Things always look like they need to be taken care of, adjusted or repositioned—nothing is wrong with that. I say, in your quest to be authentic, don't be tough on *Self.* Take care of what you can and leave the rest to God.

Understand, all are aspiring to be real and that is why many look to religion (and religious individuals) to guide them in their desire to ultimately find their reality. Some people believe it is unrealistic to be completely genuine; others believe the best they're able to achieve is to be 'seemingly' authentic and still other people just want to get along without causing raised eyebrows.

In my book *Great is thy Faithfulness* I wrote:

People are authentic when they show up without a mask or a disguise. Being authentic is not "what you see is what you get," it is, rather, "what you see was not rehearsed"; it is being aware of your true Self—no airs, no arrogances and no conceits. And, being authentic is not merely being real, for people's realities are associated with their own frame of mind, their viewpoints stem from a variety of their own emotions. You are genuine when you tell the truth; when you keep your promises; when you show up on time; when you're honest about your true feelings; when you do what you do with love. The best way to bring happiness into your life is to be your authentic *Self*.

A Spiritual Lifestyle?

Fear of criticism could make folks second guess their desire to be faithful to themselves and others. Your faithfulness is your genuine response to a call (religious or non-religious). What might people say? Will loved ones support me? What if I get it wrong? Will I be mocked as being strange? How selective should I be about the people I rely on to guide me along my spiritual path? These and other questions are what folks ask as they embark on a spiritual path. And such a path might be mire and shifting sand.

Not so long ago, I sat in a crowded auditorium listening to a prominent author talk about her new book. She began by saying… *Lots of people are walking towards the edge and don't even know this.* I gripped my jaw in astonishment. Who wants to hear that they're walking toward an edge and don't even know it? Mind you she *is* a mystery writer, nothing like me, an inspirational writer. I mention this because these days, more and more people are embracing inspirational teachings, to experience the touchy feely aspects of life.

Generally, people are optimistic. In spite of what they may be going through, many recognize that there are other happenings running concurrently which could make them change their outlook. Folks want to believe tomorrow will be, for them, a better day—a day of new possibilities. And so, as our personal world twists and turns, all of us seek ways to improve our personal wellness by participating in religious conventions, TV church, inspirational/aspirational workshops and self-help platforms.

Let me say, it is not unusual for spiritual lifestyles to morph into religious principles For example; spiritual and religious folks embrace the connection between body, mind and spirit. They acknowledge a Higher Power through worship practices and build good character as practical ways of living. And so, a variety of dogmas, teachings, verses and mantras make up a mishmash of 'clean' living.

The geneses of spirituality for many folks might be ancestry, even if fear descended on the consciousness of some at a young age.

On the one hand, folks tend to spend a lot of time micromanaging their daily life while on the other hand, folks who have accepted a spiritual alterative tend to pay attention to intuition; meaning, they allow their inner voice to direct and guide them. They embrace truth; accept honest relationships and give up 'preferred' likes because they have learned to surrender to what is important to them. A well-lit pathway is what they seek as they pursue this spiritual alterative.

As well, there are folks who resort to quick spa days, seek out retreats, time-outs, holidays, and sabbaticals. These activities may reduce stress, improve health, and increase life expectancy. However, get-a-ways are not the same as meditative contemplations for spiritual nourishment.

Meditative moments are private times folks spend in contemplation and reflection to recharge and clear their minds. Many stay in meditative states for longer rests; they make a conscious effort to *switch off* ugly *stuff* (negative thought). Others stay relaxed and doing nothing—not thinking, not talking—to experience calm. In such a state, folks might communicate on a higher level and may receive guidance and direction.

Yoga and Tai Chi are also geared toward promoting calm. These popular alternative lifestyles may be included in daily habits as reflective activities.

"Be still and know that I am God" is a biblical command— still your mind; still your body; still the need to be; and know that *stillness* is God's command to practice meditation.

When I was eleven, I was tasked to write a story titled *Myself as a Penny.*

Once upon a time, my uncle, Nickel and my Aunty Dime and I were playing in the pocket of a lovely lady. I was bright and shiny with markings and numbers written on me. Then the nice lady accidently dropped me in a puddle. I cried for a long time because I was cold and wet and my uncle and aunty were not with me. After a while the nice lady found me again, dried me off and put me in her apron pocket. I searched for my uncle and aunty but I never found them. I giggled every time the nice lady's fingers moved around my edges. Then, the nice lady took me and some of my penny friends out of her pocket. She accidently dropped me. I rolled into a crevice in the floorboard and got stuck. A little girl found me when she was sweeping the floor. She put me in her penny jar. My penny neighbours kept falling on top of me while I was in the jar and soon I was buried at the bottom of the little girl's penny jar. The end.

For a lot of folks, something happened a long time ago (or perhaps recently) to spur, if you will, a lifestyle trend. Do you remember what it was that put you on your trajectory? Do you like where you're heading?

What is your story? Is your story fear-based? Where does fear show up? In your conversations, your verses, journals, Memoirs, Special recordings? What do you gather from your personal story? Right now, at this moment, write a true story about yourself, and then put it away. Reread your story at a later date. See whether anything has changed. What has changed? Every time you tell your personal story it should be different in a positive way. Rewrite your story as often as you like until you are proud to tell your story.

In a special way, my overall writing inspiration came out of my *Penny* experience.

In this Part 4, I put forward spiritual practices to nourish the soul; the use of popular alternative lifestyles; the importance of truth telling; the significance of useful boundaries and I restate the need for lines of demarcation.

Fear of criticism could make folks second guess their desire to be faithful to themselves. Your faithfulness is your genuine response to the call to a spiritual lifestyle. What might people say? Will loved ones support me? What if I get it wrong? Will I be mocked as being strange? How selective should I be about the people I rely on to guide me along my spiritual path? These and other questions are what folks ask as they embark on a spiritual pathway.

PART FIVE

Higher Ground

*My heart has no desire to stay / Where doubts arise and fears dismay /
Though some may dwell where these abound /
My prayer, my aim, is higher ground.*

—*Johnson Oatman, Jr.*

*I want to inspire people, I want someone to look at me and say
"Because of you I didn't give up."* —Unknown.

*"Self-confidence is the most attractive quality a person can have. How
can anyone see how awesome you are if you can't see it yourself?"* —

Unknown.

WHAT DO YOU do when you are in a (negative) life-changing season and you see no way of making things better? What do you do when you are overcome with (negative) emotions? What do you do when you look for a silver lining and all you see is fog? You may choose to seek religion, which might be the safest route because of the many religious outlets and teachers available to guide you along such a path. You may choose to go the self-help way and read books with insights from psychologists and self-help gurus whose writings and collections are widely available. You may seek help from your therapist who will delve into your past and dig up things you thought you had forgotten and you may yield to your *Built-in Prayer Mechanism*, which is your spiritual advisor. (Also known as the Holy Spirit, the Comforter). Any of these routes could help you to work your way to a higher ground. And as you raise yourself up, you may find peace.

Folks who veer toward a life changing route are simply *turning over a new leaf*. Such a turning point occurs when folks look critically at their current status and choose differently. For me a change of route was surrendering everything I thought to be perfect and relying on my *Built-in Prayer Mechanism* (the Comforter) to lead, direct, and guide me.

Before we explore this Part 5 further, I need to tell you that: as a privileged child of the Most High, all your prayers are lined up and ready for you to accept as answered.

Love

Love is your smile; Love is fun and laughter; Love is hello and thank-you; Love is the name we call our spouse; Love is the name we call our children; Love is our connection to the love of others; Love is the reason we forgive ourselves; Love is how we know there are no judgements.

— And When We Pray, *Olive Rose Steele*

Let your love fly like a bird on a wing
And let your love bind you to all livin' things
And let your love shine and you'll know what I mean
That's the reason.

Let your Love Fly—Lyrics by Larry E. Williams.

Love is attachment; warmth; tenderness; acceptance of *Self* and others; a romantic liaison. Love is demonstrated in God's absolute approval. We know, from First Corinthians, Chapter 13, that love is patient, kind, not boastful, not envious, not proud, and not easily angered; doesn't behave badly and not vengeful. Still, it appears like the world is full of chaos. I say it *appears*, because when one looks closely, one sees numerous acts of love constantly bubbling up.

I truly believe all of us were born to love; be loved; to be understood and be appreciated. Some folks need to experience continuous touchy, feely affections and they will accept such affections from whomever makes it available. If they believe they've found true love, they will do everything to keep it. Hence tainted love.

True love can only be met and lived up to when folks recognize a greater love which is God's total love for everyone. His love is what puts us to sleep and wakes us up. Consider this, we may have been manipulative, rude, judgemental, and puffed-up the night before we retired to sleep, yet our Heavenly Father wakes us up to a new day and gives us another opportunity to reconcile with our world.

It is true, People who have been *burned* by love, might put up high walls (make excuses) to protect themselves from the unsavoury results of false love. Some folks find a middle ground by expressing love from a distance... they don't want to get close and risk experiencing disappointments.

Here are some examples of tainted love: erotica, pornography, prostitution and bondage. I believe those activities plant immoral pictures into minds. These imaginings might perpetuate abuses of all kinds. Banish inappropriate ideas.

If you are not feeling appropriate warmth and friendliness then know ego is raising its ugly head in the form of fear—fear of not worthy to be loved. Refuse to accommodate an uncalled-for ego when it shows up like that. In a state of true affection, you recognize a timely move to total surrender. Surrender to your loving *Self*. I am not saying that love should not be touchy-feely, I am saying touchy-feely is one part of the love experience. Know that you were given this moment to love *Self*. Be warm to your *Self*. Love is all about you; it's about where you are right now, and where you want to be in the future. Love is your destiny.

Love is our smile, Love is fun and laughter, Love is hello and thank-you; Love is the name we call our spouse; Love is the name we call our children; Love is our connection to the love of others; Love is the reason we forgive ourselves; Love is how we know there are no judgments.
—Great is Thy Faithfulness, *Olive Rose Steele*

God's absolute love is His faithfulness to humankind.

Jealousy

Yes, I know about evil, hate, jealousy, war, and so on, but those are demonstrations of love turned inside out and upside down.
—Great is thy Faithfulness, *Olive Rose Steele,*

Jealousy resides in a suspicious mind, jealousy is deep mistrust of another person's intentions; jealousy is being over-protective of someone and something for no good reason. Jealousy might even turn a loving, solid relationship into a faltering, guarded situation. Jealousy is fear raising its ugly head and showing up as envy.

Jealousy is begrudging another person's gifts, blessings, positions, finances, spouse, and happiness. Jealousy causes division. Jealousy always leads to malice, lying, cheating, stealing, and the like. Jealousy says *I have to take you down because you have something that I want.*

Jealousy makes a resentful heart weak and spiteful. Jealousy and envy cause folks to look over their shoulders continually. Jealous folks are impulsive; they might express dissatisfaction and indignation at inappropriate moments, in harmful ways. Know that jealousy in any form is not a *love thing* as some might think. Resist a Jealousy heart

Forgiveness

I always thought the strength of my character would sustain misdeeds that may come my way to upset me. And I honestly thought I had it in me to forgive anyone who was determined to hurt me. I usually make an effort to forgive the people who trespass against me even though I am angry and vengeful after every hurt. I've come to realize it is actually quite easy to forgive an offender. What? Yes.

You see, forgiveness is not about whom you forgive, it is about you and your willingness to move forward, in spite of the hurt; it is about assuring *Self* that it is okay to let go of bits and pieces of hurt that may still be lingering. Yes, if you and I are ever going to turn over a new page then we have to forgive ourselves for holding on to deep-rooted hurts and the remnants of it.

Some might say that people whom they forgive really don't deserve their forgiveness because they have willfully done them evil, know that when we forgive we say we're ready to switch gears, make a fresh start, and take the next steps. We express that we have cleansed our self of the dirt that other people heaped on us and we are ready to move forward. Do remember: nothing is right or wrong about how folks forgive therefore I encourage all to forgive to clear the way forward. And though reconciliation with the trespasser might well be the next step I say, let God take care of that.

Prayer

People pray for calm and inner peace, for family and friends, to receive miracles, to fulfill spiritual obligations and to assuage fear.
—Great is thy Faithfulness, *Olive Rose Steele*

Prayer is desire, plea, supplication, petition and appeal for Divine involvement. Many people pray to experience a personal relationship with a Higher Power and for continuous spiritual growth. Folks pray for things they need; things they don't need; for the needs of family and friends; to be exonerated, and even for justice on behalf of people they don't even know. As well, folks pray when they're in a bind;

when others are in a bind; when they lose something; to give thanks for favours and for blessings. Whatever the situation, our communication with the Divine through prayer will keep us grounded. We might be alerted to stay put or carry on, based on our prayer or we might receive an instant miracle.

When you pray, you give up your desire to be in control of your circumstances; you make a decision to release all outcomes, and you tell your *Self* there is no more room in our heart for doubt. God listens to every prayer. Surrender negative thoughts that hold you back and cast every burden on the Christ within.

Our father which art in heaven
Hallowed be thy name
Thy kingdom come, thy will be done on earth
as it is in heaven
Give us this day our daily bread
And forgive us our debts, as we forgive our debtors
And lead us not into temptation, but deliver us from evil
For thine is the kingdom and the power and the glory forever
and ever—Matthew 6: 9-13

The foregoing prayer is known as the Lord's Prayer. It is a fundamental prayer that is recited in many settings and on numerous occasions. The Lord's Prayer covers every aspects of human life—worship, protection, mealtime, shelter, forgiveness (ourselves and others), debts, dos, don'ts and desires and victory. This is the prayer that Jesus taught his followers, however, as His followers develop a relationship with the One to whom they pray, they begin to express the contents of their hearts in their own words in a personal way. Folks should know prayer is constant—a 24/7 activity. Say your prayer with purpose, continually. Believe in the awesome power of your prayer and have faith in Divine response.

Answered Prayers

Big, bold, grand, answered prayers are on record. For example, reversed life-threatening illnesses, rectified finances, reconciled relationships, freed captives and spiritual turnarounds are just some remarkable 'answered' prayers. On the other hand, the convenient parking spot close to your doctor's office, the 50% discount on your new pair of walking shoes and the coupon you received for a free coffee, should also be considered answered prayers. Answered prayers challenge people's awareness.

It is true, folks receive blessings and favor all the time and many believe these occurrences were pulled together by their hard work; and yes, that may have something to do with it. That might be the reason some folks exhibit an amount of superiority and arrogance in the management of their answered prayers, even if those prayers (blessings) came about through celestial powers. I'm not saying it is wrong to acknowledge your input and hard work, I am proposing a way which might be wide-reaching and compassionate.

What kind of a giver are you? Does success makes you haughty? Do you squander your blessings? Do you manage your responsibilities in a kind-hearted way?

If you are in the middle of a personal 'do-over' and there is a pause in the flow of your blessings, refer to the law of giving and receiving. See how the more you give, the more you will get back.

Remember, give generously from your answered prayers. Show concerns for folks who don't have, so you'll always receive continuous flow. Don't be floored when your prayers *dry up*—it might be a signal to give more from your answered prayers.

Reconciliation

Reconciliation involves compromise; an effort to restore a satisfying relationship. The work of reconciliation is usually necessary after forgiveness. And this might be awkward because even after folks resolved a difference, understanding why things turned out the way they did remain uncertain.

When I think about reconciliation, I immediately recall an occurrence involving my cousin Thelma. Thelma left me stranded at a picnic (in an unfamiliar town) when we were children. I admit, she did come back and apologise. I grudgingly forgave Thelma. (Observe how the incident is seared in my memory).

For many, it might be easier to forgive another person's carelessness and move on; however it may take a longer time to reconcile ill feelings.

Reconciliation demands an amount of humility from the individuals involved and this always slows down the process. (Not all parties will be ready to reunite at the same time) But those who are ready for reconciliation are ready to yield to Divine Spirit within. They are ready to walk the path to redemption. Folks should not be hard on Self if reconciliation is coming slowly; be merciful to *Self*. Be reminded that your ego is ever present, prompting you to stand up for yourself.

Redemption

My late Nana had a go-to place deep in her heart. She talked about that place as her redemption ground; a place of forgiveness and reunion; a place to make amends; a place where her festering wounds (doubt, suspicion, hatred, malice) are allowed to breathe and be healed; a place to connect on a personal level with Spirit within. Nana told me she came away from her redemption ground assured of God's favor. What a wonderful feeling that must have been!

Redemption ground was a tougher place for me. I had a difficult time surrendering my fears (doubt, suspicion, hurt, disgust) so that I could be healed.

I had been standing at a junction. Didn't know which path to take although I recognized that my hope for relief must come through self-improvement; all of the guilt that fear had piled on me had become burdensome. Fear of every kind over took me. I got down on my knees at redemption ground and prayed. I came away from that place feeling relieved of burdens I'd been carrying for a long time. How? I relinquished every thought, every feeling, every action I had believed to be right and yielded to Divine Spirit within for direction and guidance. I surrendered my arrogant ego at a place of repose. I shook off the dirt other people heaped on me and I stepped on to a solid rock knowing I had nothing to fear. A makeover was taking place.

I can see clearly now the rain is gone,
I can see all obstacles in my way,
Gone are the dark clouds that had me blind
It's gonna be a bright (bright) bright sunshiny day
—I Can See – Jimmy Cliff

Don't feel like you have to revisit your redemption ground every time fear tackles you. Redemption shows you're being made over; redemption points toward *square one*. Enter your redemption ground with an open heart and walk away knowing you're being made over, with God's help.

Feelings

I want to acknowledge everyone who might be feeling hurt at this very moment; you might be feeling hurt because of the doings of spouse, children, family members and friends. At this very moment, you might not be feeling happy and whole. You may even feel that your Heavenly Father has abandoned you. You're probably asking yourself: *Can I trust my feelings?* Yes. Feelings are emotions that only appear when you put them into action. Feelings are good and bad. I say, reason with your feelings before you lean on them for feelings come and feelings go. Your feelings are as bad (and as good) as you want them to be. It is a strong-willed person who does not get carried away by bad feelings.

Folks may experience bad feelings when they're out of work; they've been lied about, lied to, belittled, ignored on purpose, misjudged, and told to sit down and shut up. Like me, you probably don't remember the root cause of your bad feelings. I say, excuse yourself for even trying to remember where it all started. And while you're at it, excuse the people who caused you to conjure up the bad feelings in the first place. Dismiss bad feeling.

It is true, bad feelings have a root cause—usually there's something sitting in our psyche, something unresolved, which was never forgiven or forgotten.

Bad feelings appear as disrespect, apathy; not good enough and those bad feelings take a longer time to go away. I too have had those feelings—even a compliment used to sound disrespectful to me! On the other hand, folks have experienced great joys, delightful relationships and extended happiness, and those are good feelings—delight in them.

Banish every negative feeling that is holding you back and start feeling happy, healthy, and beautiful (handsome). Shake off bad feelings and watch good feelings appear. When folks put a positive spin on how they feel their mood changes, their point of view is different and their responses sound better.

Confidence

Confidence is boldness, confidence says you know where you're going and you have a plan to get there. Your confidence not only inspires you, it inspires your family, colleagues, friends, and onlookers. Confidence attracts meaningful relationships. Confidence shows a balanced life.

Take stock. Think about your life so far; list the stuff you've accumulated (tangible stuff and soul stuff). Think through the steps you need to take in order to implement meaningful change where necessary. Write them down. Stay with it. In the beginning you may want to keep your thoughts to yourself. Doubt and negative self-talk can destroy your confidence. Let your mind stay on positive thoughts with clear visualizations. Be discriminating about offensive interpretations, avoid uninvited participation in other people's business, resist other people's objectionable opinions and stay in an atmosphere of boldness. Remember, you will not always see everything other folks do as spiritual, however with confidence you will make sound decisions that will keep your stuff in proper order.

Truth

"My truth is my authentic self: it is the opposite of a fib, a lie and every falsehood I ever engaged. My truth supersedes any doctrine, dogma or belief that was ever shown to me."

—And When We Pray, *Olive Rose Steele*

Your truth is in your moment. Truth is what may be happening in real time and how you are reacting to it. So, what is your truth? Are you still seething over your divorce? Are you single and struggling to raise your children? Is the job your Achilles heel? Would it make sense to change course now? Truth is not always pretty or even what most of us would like it to be. I say, own it. If it is happening to you, it belongs to you. Unless you own your (confront) truth, you won't be able to deal with it. I know that dealing with truth can be ugly. For the hardest part about owning truth is when we are pressed by Spirit within to rectify (correct) our truth. Know that accepting untruth will stymie the dreams of folks. Change untruth to truth.

There was a time when my truth meant I was standing on solid ground, that is to say, I had everything I desired. I was the captain of my own ship and nothing or no one could stop my progress. Then the day came when I began to wobble. There were instances where I felt I was sinking in mire. My belief in myself plunged and my so-called world spun in mire for a long time.

I admit my desire to stand strong during those challenging times was haughty. During those times I continued to say things were fine (accepting (un)truth as truth). My favourite phrase was "I'm fine." Sure, but I didn't have a roof over my head. How fine was that? Right then I knew I had to change some (so called) truths—start over. I swallowed my pride and started again.

People close to us can usually tell when some things are not quite okay. For example, when your telephone suddenly gets disconnected; when you're looking for a loan from family or friends to pay the rent or mortgage and when there's no food on the dinner table for your children. Those are facts that say the ground on which you stand is shaky. Folks notice. Assess the ground on which you stand. Move to a higher ground.

You may need to shed some heavy, unwanted *stuff*. If you are burdened with other people's stuff—let it go. You may need to go back to your personal basics and take another look at your own *stuff*. See what you can discard. See what is worth keeping. Know that there is always another way to do things. There is no shame in being honest with you.

I said at the beginning of this book that I'm a work in progress; I am being moulded and made over every single day, being honest with myself is important to me.

Up to a few years ago, I thought everything I'd been doing was good even when some of the *good* things were not working for me. Then I learned to accept the things I cannot change, change the things I could, and leave the rest to God. Truth will take on a whole new meaning when you own it in the way it shows up.

Don't be concerned about the friends you may need to avoid—take it from me, they'll avoid you first! And that is not a bad thing.

Dear God

Please help me to understand and live my truth

Guide me to perfect realities, and when my feet are off the ground as they are today, fill my mind with common sense

Plant my feet on solid ground

I ask these mercies in Jesus' name

—Olive Rose Steele

Walk

I never said that you should walk through brick walls or even that you should walk on water.

I am the Door, *Paul Ferrini*

What comes to mind when you think: *Walk*?

A Walk is the manner of putting one foot in front of the other; a combination of carefully chosen turns along a path; forward strides. As well, a walk might be described as a committed spiritual practice or a lifestyle change.

Walk, as a spiritual practice is a series of focussed, thoughtful steps that promotes peaceful living and encourages faith. This practice brings folks closer to true Self, and might even point them to gifts and talents that lay dormant in their nature. No doubt, folks will experience a variety of emotions during their walk—fear, resentment, failure, un-forgiveness, to name a few. Don't let emotional interruptions stymie your way of walking; no one is perfect.

Your emotions are tools from life's tool box for you to use as necessary. Emotions indicate to you which ones to keep and which ones to banish. You're paying attention to your emotions because you want to live in unity with *Self* and others. Don't beat up on yourself during those emotional walk. Such emotions are your ego nature seeking love. Look deeply at negative thoughts and emotions; observe how emotions pull and push to get your attention as you walk.

Honour your emotions by deciding which ones you really want to keep and keep emotions that make you feel good. Banish emotions that make you sad, miserable and depressed.

As you walk, you will be required to deal with the fragile ego of other people in a loving way. Consider that your brothers and sisters bring with them their own emotions. Your kind words of love may be what they've been waiting on to inspire them on their journey. It is true, we live in a complex world; a world that requires us to live in harmony with other people. Still, our walk could become challenging if harmony is lopsided. In moments of lopsided harmony we are required to give more of ourselves.

Every moment of our walk is a moment to give love.

Points of View

People who don't bother to put forward a point of view should know that life will assign a point of view that may not suit their purpose.

—Great is Thy Faithfulness, *Olive Rose Steele*

A point of view is the boldness with which folks put forward their ideas; it is the manner in which they make their approach; it is their expressions.

Some points of view might be sensitive because of the personal nature of the remarks. People might say your point of view is just that... the way you understand and put forward a narrative.

What is your point of view? Is your point of view *your* honest opinion? Is your point of view contingent upon another person's opinions? I say, express your point of view, for it might be relevant. Know that your point of view is an ally of your opinion.

As you recognize *Self* and others in a significant way, your point of view might change or might become your core principle. Honour your point of view.

I am sometimes skittish when I'm asked where I stand on certain matters. Such questions often push me to give decisive answers or give clear opinions and I'm usually cautious with my opinions.

Have a point of view.

Reason

This might be strange, but it is true, everyone has a reason for doing what they do; whether to be present, to participate, to quit, to be happy, or to be sad. And the reason is usually for their self-interest.

Poor Me: Folks are usually moved by sad stories and there are no shortages of people who will play the sympathy card in a selfish way, to get what they desire. I am talking about the *poor me* people; the *feeling put down* people; the *abused and abandoned* people. They will tug at your heartstrings to get your money, your sympathy and your goodwill, and they rarely empathise with you or your story. If selfishness is what drives your reason you will lose out on the goodwill that folks might extend to you.

I am scared: I admit, I have been in and out of the *I am scared* category many times. A big fright for me is fear of theme park rides. (I will only do the merry-go-round rides). For many folks, **I am scared** to travel by plane is their big fright. I truly believe the real reason that many folks are scared to travel by plane is because they are scared of dying. (Most might not admit to this). If fear is what is driving your reason—banish fear.

For many folks, their reason is an aim, a goal, an end result. Your reason might very well be what's driving you to a finishing point at this very moment. For what reason you do what you do? On what basis do you do what you do? What is driving your actions? What results do you expect when you do what you do? Will you benefit from what you do?

Everyone has a reason and an agenda for doing what they do. Take stock, be truthful, no excuses. Putting the responsibility for not having a reason on somebody else is unfair. Let your reason be your aim, your purpose, your intention and your desired result.

Awareness

Awareness is much more than being mindful or even alert. For example, you and I are generally aware of what is happening in our moments; we are informed about the other folks in our space. We look at *Self* without criticizing or judging; we observe every incident, every disappointment and every triumph, and we accept slipups as legitimate mistakes.

Priests, Pastors, Imams, Faith Leaders and those who operate in an atmosphere of piety are tasked to show an amount of sensitivity in their mindfulness of other people's plight. Generally, folks tend to close their eyes to emotional mannerisms (sad, angry, fearful, jealous) and recognize the survivor, sufferer and victim. Therefore, with the awareness of people's troubles many believe they might grow and develop mentally, emotionally and spiritually and I tend to agree.

Hope

First Corinthians 13:13, chronicles Faith, Hope and Charity. It says that the greatest of the three virtues is Charity. People mostly deliberate on *Faith* (belief, conviction, trust) and *Charity* (love, friendship, offering, donations, and gifts) and less consideration is given to *Hope*.

What are you hoping for? Like many, you might be hoping for success of a certain kind, might be hoping to be married, have children and live a blissful life.

Hope a necessary quality. Hope is actually what most people turn to when circumstances go awry. Hope encourages folks to look forward to results that are to their liking. Hope fosters positive thinking and inspires confidence in a bright future. I've noticed people expressing a hopeless existence; they've lost hope in realizing a dream; repairing a marriage, children, and personal relationships.

As a necessary spiritual armour, Hope encourages your readiness to deal with the issues of life as they appear. Hope may not always operate to your liking and that is when folks say their hope is *dash*—and then they give up. *Dashed* hope usually occurs when folks put their confidence in an outcome that did not happen on their timeline; and yet hope implies there is a light at the end of the tunnel; things will be better. Have a positive outlook; it inspires you to keep on hoping.

Be courageous, move forward with confidence in the fact that your faith is truly aligned with the things you hope for. Hope to be happy and healthy. Look with anticipation and expectation. Your hope should be built on nothing less than anticipation. Hope means keeping your dreams alive.

Clarification

Clarification is really additional information to fully grasp what you're feeling and hearing. You and I might hear the same message yet we understand it differently. I can say, there will be times when Spirit within will give information that some of us will not fully understand—not immediately. If you think you're hearing a message from the heart but you don't understand the meaning or the way forward I suggest you yield to Spirit within for an explanation.

Clarification can come to folks in different ways. For example, clarification might pop out from a book; comments from a stranger; meditative visualizations and inspirational words from a friend or mentor—all of the above might shed light on your way forward. Intuitively, you will know when you've received clarification.

When I was prompted to let go of what I was holding, I truly did not understand the instruction. I was not aware that I was holding anything—except my thoughts and feelings. Was I being instructed to write down what was coming from my heart? When in doubt, seek clarification.

My clarification unfolded in this way: First I was moved to journalize my prayers, and then I was prompted to record my emotional state in the moments of my prayers. The end result was my book titled *And When We Pray*.

Order

Order is not always a command; a ranking; an ultimatum or even lining things up. Order is priority and importance; order encourages stillness and allows simplicity. At crucial points all should pause and bring order to stuff that is falling out of place, be it in spirit, mind, body and affairs.

We've talked about stuff that could make our way foggy, now let's line them up so we can see clearly: Set aside ample space for *You*. Plan activities—job, family, friends, love, meditate, pray. Organize time for play, recreation, exercise, nutrition and repose.

When you've done all of the above, the fog should have lifted. No? Did you say you've done all you can and still the sun wont shine through? Yes? Then there must be clutter lying around. Where is the clutter?—in boxes at a storage facility? Strewn about in the basement of your residence? In the attic? Stuffed in drawers? Closets? Under your bed? Where is the stuff that is causing you grief? Are you happy with the order in which you place your stuff? Is your stuff open for all to see? If so, will just looking at them make you frown on your mess? Start over. Turn the 'page'. Put your stuff in order. Organize your basement, closets and drawers; throw out (donate) unwanted clothes, shoes and knickknack. Ask God to show you what to do with the spiritual stuff.

Evil

Most folk will agree that evil is bad, cruel, hateful, malicious, wicked—all of those behaviours. So who or what is *evil?* Definitions of evil vary; however, in this context I will say evil is the opposite of good. The devil is generally recognized as the carrier of evil. Some might disagree that the devil has anything to do with evil or there is even an entity called the devil, but since I'm not a Theologian I'll leave details on theology to religious scribes.

Folks identify things that happen to them as good and evil. I say evil is a sham; Evil might seem real and will *take* root in a mind that's starved for self-confidence.

Following are some opinions: Evil is within humankind. Evil is recognized and talked about as unfriendly. Trusted folks might give evil feedbacks. Evil knows that folks will ensure its place in their personal space. Evil is always seeking out new ways of messing up people's heads and making them change course for no reason. Evil feels your pain.

I might be wrong, nevertheless, I say, the above are points of view to be debated.

This is what I believe; anything that is not of love is evil.

Don't stand around and watch as evil destroys your health, your family, your relationships, your children, and your finances. And don't be surprise to learn that evil deeds are additional ways that fear raises its ugly head. As soon as you recognize evil, call it by the name it presents itself, put on your prayer armour then banish evil into oblivion where it belongs. Watch how it cowers and withdraws when it recognizes you as an armoured child of God. No matter the negatives which are occurring in your moment, don't be distracted by them, rely on Divine guidance; stay clear of other people's advice and opinions. If you believe the negatives to be evil it will overwhelm your thinking.

Always remember, evil will enter the minds of innocent folks in the form of fear—banish evil into oblivion when it raises its ugly head.

Eyes are always watching

You know this is my favorite catchphrase (*Eyes are always watching*). Folks should know that in every moment of time someone, somewhere, is noticing them!

People come and go; doing this and doing that; observing occurrences and making decisions. Eyes stay longer on appealing objects and people; eyes stay fascinated by movements and colours; eyes are captivated by entertaining activities.

Since the world is in continuous movement and involves people from all walks of life and since we may not know which information folks may take away when they exit our sphere of influence, we ought to stay aware. The following is my personal account.

I was sitting in a coffee shop sipping my morning coffee when a young man walked up to my table and asked my permission to sit on the empty seat beside me. Fine. He struck up a conversation. I accommodated. Five minutes later, I was his counsellor, his healer, and his therapist. I happened to have had a copy of my book *And When We Pray* in my purse. I gave him the copy. He rose to leave when another young man came into my presence holding out a twenty-dollar note. He reminded me that sometime ago; he had taken one of my books and had not yet paid for it. Great!

Before I exited the coffee shop, a woman walked up to me and marveled at the brightness of my expression. These folks were strangers to me; however, something about my actions attracted their attention. Know that you and I could be used in any moment to reveal the 'miracle' that another person prayed for. Folks ought to pay attention to goings-on around them and react to what gives hope and encouragement.

Highfalutin—what is it?

I first heard the word Highfalutin when I was just a young girl and it stuck in my memory. To be Highfalutin is to be self-important, showy and pretentious. It is when folks put value on attainment and mannerisms that say they are okay because they are superior. They highlight their status, hang out with the 'right' people, 'name drop' to show who they know and maintain memberships in named social clubs.

It becomes convoluted when highfalutin folks come into your domain with their highfalutinism and wishes you to fit in to their style. Why do *I* need to know this, you ask?

Highfalutinism carries with it extra *stuff*. *I* am suggesting folks choose simplicity over highfalutinism. I do believe that with good principles and accurate information you and I can experience a healthy, stress free life and enjoy satisfying personal relationships.

Gift(s)/Talent(s)

Love comes from him, because he has received the gift and learned to give it unconditionally to all who would receive it
—I am the Door, *Paul Ferrini*

Generally, folks think of gifts as benevolence—favour, hand-outs, donations, and keepsakes. For this section, we'll talk about gifts as talents which were divinely given to serve each another. Gifts/talents are what the world would be devoid of if folks did not make them available. My favourite question to ask is: *What is that one thing you would love to do, the talent that would bring you joy, the skill you would work at 24/7 and then give it away with love, but you push it to the back of your mind?*

I believe someone's gifts/talents are tied to his or her purpose. Your gift/talent is something you do every waking hour and quite often you give it away; it is that thing you know you are purposed to do; it is the thing that brings you total joy and satisfaction. For example, you are a nurse but you've always wanted to be a painter. You are a teacher but you've always wanted to be a preacher you are a bodyguard but you've always wanted to be a writer. You are a lawyer because your talent is in defending folks. Then there are people who waver before deciding to pursue a gift/talent that they truly love; I say, the fact that the gift/talent is in your heart, means you should vigorously pursue it because that could very well be your calling.

Appreciate your gifts/talents; use them to honour each another. Be unwavering in your desire to succeed at what your heart is calling you to do. Fear of condemnation and criticism might enter your thinking. Fear is a liar, refuse to believe the lies fear tells. Do not dishonour the relevance of your gifts/talents out of fear that people may be jealous; fear could confuse your mind; move forward with determination!

If you're aiming to stand on firm ground then you should be steadfast in developing your gifts/talents. You might have to crawl through shifting sand so be ready to inspire your *Self*. Know that there will be times when your only motivation is your belief in *self*.

It occurred to me that folks needed to hear what I had to say and if I were ever going to be authentic I had to give my gift/talent generously. I use my gift/talent to *illuminate* folks in a special way; recognize Divine Spirit in other people; encourage hearts to put into practice what they know; speak truth to the heart that is receptive and extend my true emotions without feeling inhibited. I truly believe my inspirational thoughts are what folks need to hear.

I don't know where your experiences are leading you right now but I can tell you this, I spent a lot of years going around in circles thinking I was using my gift/talent, until I heeded the call to put my thoughts in writing.

In the past, I thought gifts/talents were exclusively for religious people. See Romans 12: 6-8 and Corinthians 12: 8-10 for a list of gifts/talents. Later, I found out that gifts are given in different ways, for special reasons. Do you know what your gifts/talents are? Could you give away your gifts/talents with love?

All of us carry something special with us when we were born and we're mandated to leave something special behind when we take leave of this life. Boldly express your gifts/talents.

Staying alive

We're empowered, feeling strong. We're ready to take steps that will lead us out of our perceived mire. I say *perceived* mire because most of what we see with our naked eyes is not the whole truth. The truth is we can change our thoughts, words and actions, which will invite trusting, respectful connections for a happy, healthy wholesome future. We really don't have to continue on a path that we don't like or enjoy.

I have told you this before: be aware of negative folks. You know the ones I'm talking about—they could be spouses, family, friends, colleagues and folks you recently met. Know who they are so that you can deal with their egos. I'm not talking about folks who are genuinely in need of your backing. I'm talking about people who fill your ears with negative (ego) talk; the chronic whiners and nit-pickers; the folks who frequently seek your assistance to help them survive their poor choices. Help them if you can but get as far away as possible from chronic moaning. Don't 'play' mind games with other people's ego.

Since you know there will be stumbling blocks to look out for, valleys to go through, and mountains to go around, then you must be prepared to face these obstacles (I suggest you give these obstacles fear based names) and then banish them into oblivion as you go forward. You most likely have to confess some hurts to your *Self* (or to a sister or a brother) and forgive some trespassers so that you can cleanse your soul of the dregs of fear. All the same, you are changing to a behaviour pattern that will produce a different result for you; you're on a path to *Self* recovery. And other people might see you as weird because of your decision to walk in love—go ahead, make the decision today. Stay alive!

Next Step

Your next step might be back to *square one*. Let's start with this well-known, simple children's prayer:

Gentle Jesus / Meek and mild / Look upon a little child / Pity my simplicity / Suffer me to come to thee.
—*Charles Wesley.*

For many folks, the next step may come after a graduation, marriage, break-up, divorce, a significant birth day and the demise of a loved one. In the hustle and bustle of everyday living, folks are tempted with a string of emotions—doubt and fear are just two of many. Yes, it is true that challenges are everyday occurrences, however, we *must* believe that we are already given everything we need to survive this life, plus we have a Powerful Divine Spirit within us to direct and lead us every step of our way. Still, the next step could be slow and painful, that is because, fear (of all sorts) bars folks from accepting a helping hand when they miss a step. No matter where you're standing at this moment, know that with help you can go to a higher ground.

You may be going through crappy challenges and you might be searching for a firm grip, take the help that is being handed to you; take the next step. I know the feeling of sinking sand and I know it is not a wonderful place to be. Don't let fear hinder you from taking that next step.

New day

You and I have been on an exploration; a search, if you will, for *the* reason—the reason we're alive at this moment; the reason we are loved in spite of our faults; the reason we are healthy and whole even when we neglect *Self*; the reason we're all that we desire and we're still not satisfied.

We are complex beings. Our journey is endless. Endless you say? Yes, because our experiences are new in every moment and they take us to places where we identify with no one except God and Self.

For most people, a new day is when they wake up from a reasonable number of hours sleep to the sight of the morning sun. For others, a new day is an awakening—a sudden knowledge, a change in thinking, a new release, a different way of living. And for some people, their new day will be the day they stare down fear and call it the name it shows up as; the day they tell their ego they are no longer at its beck and call; the day they surrender everything they believe to be right and cast all their burdens on Spirit within and go free.

Those who are willing to start *a new day* should know that it won't be easy; negative thoughts will tell you it is not wise to throw everything you know as real out the window and begin on a path you never walked. Doubt will seem pragmatic, fear will make sense and you will question a *foolish* stance you've decided to take. You surrendered. You've given up stuff you've been dragging around; you've relinquished your role as a sounding board and you're in harmony with life as it presents. Know that your willingness to devote time and energy to a new way of walking for the rest of your life will be challenged or even ridiculed.

Some people have experienced a personal relationship with God; they recognize the spiritual being that they truly are and have incorporated fundamental values in worship and communion for their wellbeing. A new day signifies new hopes—a desire to *live*, to try again, to laugh again.

It's your Turn

You have a fair idea about the expression *My Stuff, Your Stuff* and *Our Stuff*. You're okay with the term: wholesome relationships. You appreciate and value the things that changed around you—a spouse's solid support; a child's genuine show of respect; unified family; co-operative friends; demonstrated authenticity and most importantly, YOU are peaceful.

Now it is your turn. You're ready to tell your *Self* the truth about who you truly are. You are ready to say you're happy, healthy, loving, and whole. You're ready to set realistic goals; pull your *soul stuff* together and leave negative people and experiences behind. You have a good sense of where you're heading and perhaps on which ground you'd like to stand. Your ego is watching you. Ego thinks you've lost your mind. Ego will quickly remind you of the bad feelings you've endured; that you should look out for yourself. Ego will insist you stand up for yourself though you're sure the change will take you to a better place—a solid ground. Ego will continue to prompt you into action when you're mocked or when you're labelled weak because of your new point of view. But you will stand your ground, you will banish fear, and its cohorts (doubt, indecision, worry and all of the other ones) into oblivion where they belong. You're moving forward on a positive path, you cannot stop now. Play the mind game with your own mind, tell your mind it is yours to change as you desire. Remind your mind of its split personality—Ego and *Self.* Decide on *Self,* look how your life becomes different as you yield to *Self!*

Based on what we've discussed, I designed the following questions to inspire confidence in your way forward. I call this exercise *TRUTH EXERCISE.* It is intended to chart thoughts, habits, points of view and future directions. It allows you to pause and look internally to see how your thoughts connect with your external circumstances As with any new endeavour, you will need to set aside valuable time for this procedure. Now as you begin to work through the questions, write down honest answers. Don't feel you have to answer all the questions at one sitting. Keep your written answers for as long as you wish (days, weeks, months) in a private place. Revisit your answers; let your original answers stay, write new ones (don't erase your original answers, not quickly). Recognize that change is sometimes a slow process. Your hopes, your dreams and everything in-between may surface in most unusual ways. Don't be hard on yourself—you're slowly changing.

Start by giving spontaneous answers, then move to deep-thinking, thoughtful answers. Revise an answer as often as you wish. You will discover new things about *you*.

NOW ...Close your eyes and look inward before you attempt to answer these questions. What is the one (or two, or three, however many) thing that is foremost on your mind? Open your eyes; write it down. Go to the Truth Exercise questions start answering them, one after the other.

READY …..SET …… GO

TRUTH EXERCISE

Take an inventory of your *stuff*—tangibles and *soul stuff* (write them down).

....
....
....
....
....
....
....
....
....
....
....
....
....
....
....
....
....
....
....
....

Are you truly happy with all of your stuff? Does your stuff weigh you down?

....

....

....

....

....

....

....

....

....

....

....

Are you assured that you have the right stuff?

....

....

....

....

....

....

....

....

....

....

Which stuff is essential to you? Why?

....
....
....
....
....
....
....
....
....
....
....
....

Could you live without any of your stuff?

....
....
....
....
....
....
....
....
....
....
....
....

What stuff do you share with others?

....
....
....
....
....
....
....
....
....
....
....
....

Are your decisions fear-based? Why? What is the reason you
do what you do?

....
....
....
....
....
....
....
....
....
....

Who is affected by what you do?

....

....

....

....

....

....

....

....

....

....

....

....

How do people (in general) react to what you do?

....

....

....

....

....

....

....

....

....

....

....

What results do you expect when you do what you do?

....
....
....
....
....
....
....
....
....
....
....
....

Will you benefit from what you do?

....
....
....
....
....
....
....
....
....
....
....

Your hope is built on what?

....
....
....
....
....
....
....
....
....
....
....
....

Are you standing on solid footing?

....
....
....
....
....
....
....
....
....
....
....

Where I'm standing, hope is my strength. Explain.

....

....

....

....

....

....

....

....

....

....

....

Where I'm standing I have no worries. Why?

....

....

....

....

....

....

....

....

....

....

....

....

Where I'm standing I am not alone. Explain.

....
....
....
....
....
....
....
....
....
....
....

Where I'm standing I trust that all my needs will be met. Explain.

....
....
....
....
....
....
....
....
....
....
....

Where I'm standing I can make up my own mind about Faith, Hope, and Love. Explain.

. . . .

. . . .

. . . .

. . . .

. . . .

. . . .

. . . .

. . . .

. . . .

. . . .

Where I'm standing I know I'm the best that I can be. Why?

. . . .

. . . .

. . . .

. . . .

. . . .

. . . .

. . . .

. . . .

. . . .

. . . .

. . . .

Where I'm standing I am confident in God's love. Explain.

....
....
....
....
....
....
....
....
....
....
....

Where I'm standing I can testify to God's unconditional love. Explain.

....
....
....
....
....
....
....
....
....
....
....

Where I'm standing I have nothing to be ashamed of. How come?

....
....
....
....
....
....
....
....
....
....

Where I am standing now I can acknowledge the truth about my *Self*, Why?

....
....
....
....
....
....
....
....
....
....
....

Beginning right now I resolve to be authentic to *Self* and resist fear in all its forms because…

....

....

....

....

....

....

....

....

....

....

Starting today I will seek, accept and live the truth about my *Self* because….

....

....

....

....

....

....

....

....

....

....

....

Starting today I will trust that the results I expect when I pray will show up because...

....

....

....

....

....

....

....

....

....

....

Starting today I will not add thought, word or deed to other people's business because...

....

....

....

....

....

....

....

....

....

....

....

I will be peaceful, beginning today because…

. . . .

. . . .

. . . .

. . . .

. . . .

. . . .

. . . .

. . . .

. . . .

. . . .

. . . .

. . . .

From now on I choose to be aware of all that's occurring around me because…

. . . .

. . . .

. . . .

. . . .

. . . .

. . . .

. . . .

. . . .

. . . .

. . . .

Beginning today, I will banish fear from my heart because...

....

....

....

....

....

....

....

....

....

....

....

From this moment on I will have fun at everything I do because God wants me to be happy. If you are certain of that, then say why...

....

....

....

....

....

....

....

....

....

....

I will now surrender my toxic emotions (name them). Why?

....

....

....

....

....

....

....

....

....

....

....

I will set manageable boundaries. Why?

....

....

....

....

....

....

....

....

....

....

....

....

I can see clearly. Explain.

....
....
....
....
....
....
....
....
....
....
....

I am ready to own up to my neglect of Self and forgive myself for doing so. Explain.

....
....
....
....
....
....
....
....
....
....
....

I will own my mistakes and try to make fewer? Why?

....
....
....
....
....
....
....
....
....
....
....
....

I will not deny joy in my life. Why?

....
....
....
....
....
....
....
....
....
....
....
....

What three things do you allow to upset your peace? Explain.

....

....

....

....

....

....

....

....

....

....

....

Questions YOU ask *Self*.

....

....

....

....

....

....

....

....

....

....

....

....

Answers *Self* gives YOU.

. . . .

. . . .

. . . .

. . . .

. . . .

. . . .

. . . .

. . . .

. . . .

. . . .

. . . .

Come back to your TRUTH EXERCISE as often as you like. See if your outlook on *Self* has changed. You may decide you want to update your answers. Never discard your original answers for your aim is to track your progress.

Prioritize, Prioritize, Prioritize

In this concluding Section we refresh our thinking on Self— *My Self, Your Self* and *Our Self.* We understand *Self* as the 'I am' of who we are.

I rant about *Ego* and its disguises.

Fear is the enemy.

In the final analysis, your experiences are your calls. Now, you might want to prioritize the *stuff* that is important to you so that you can fully enjoy this new way of walking. Some folks might require additional information after they've read this book. Have no fear, information will come to you when you have need.

Here are some things I discovered about me after I completed my own TRUTH EXERCISE: The wisdom, peace, love and happiness that I seek is within me; everything that had occurred and will occur in my life was and will be my wish; my desires have always allowed my good, my bad, and my ugly. I will always be at the rudder of my ship; I will always call my shots. My feelings of harassment, disrespect, and being passed over, are my perceptions.

Now you know, your challenges might well be same as mine. Here's the good news, you can begin to choose your steps. You can review your walk, if and when you miss a step or two. Your new way of walking is your business, you're not required to announce your business to friends and family; or anyone, for that matter. Your disposition will materialise in a perfect way.

Congratulations, you now know a lot about the greatest person on this planet – YOU!

Prayer of St. Francis of Assisi

Lord make me an instrument of Your peace;

Where there is hatred, let me sow love;

Where there is injury, pardon;

Where there is error, the truth;

Where there is doubt, the faith;

Where there is despair, hope;

Where there is darkness, light;

Where there is sadness, joy;

O Divine Master; Grant that I may not so much seek

To be consoled, as to console;

To be understood, as to understand;

To be loved, as to love;

For it is in giving that we receive;

It is in pardoning, that we are pardoned.

The Serenity Prayer

God grant me the serenity

to accept the things I cannot change;

courage to change the things I can;

and wisdom to know the difference

Living one day at a time;

Enjoying one moment at a time;

Accepting hardships as the pathway to peace;

Taking, as He did, this sinful world

as it is, not as I would have it;

Trusting that He will make all things right

if I surrender to His Will;

That I may be reasonably happy in this life

and supremely happy with Him

Forever in the next

Amen

—Reinhold Niebuhr

Psalms 23 as a Prayer

The Lord is my Shepherd I shall not want

He maketh me to lie down in green pastures

He leadeth me beside the still waters

He restoreth my soul; He leadeth me in the path of

righteousness for His name sake

Yea, though I walk through the valley of the shadow of death

I will fear no evil; for thou are with me; thy rod and thy staff

they comfort me

Thou preparest a table before me in the presence of my

enemies; thou anointest my head with oil; my cup runeth over

Surely goodness and mercy shall follow me all the days of my

life and I will dwell in the house of the lord for ever.

Dear God

With hands clasped, we enter Your Light

We leave at the door everything we believe to be right

We confess all negative thoughts and feelings

We embrace Your Divine Spirit within us

Purify our hearts and renew our spirits

Give us understanding, peace and love

Show mercy and heal our spiritual and physical pain

Shine Your White Light upon us, Dear God

And Illuminate our consciousness

As we seek refuge in this special place

And so be it.

—*Olive Rose Steele*

God our Heavenly Father

We give You thanks for this moment

Your sons and daughters have come together in love

For a meeting of our hearts and minds

Bind us in perfect harmony

Show us Your plan

Let everything we say and do be to Your honor and glory

We love You

We adore You

We honor Your presence

We sing Your praise

We thank you for Your goodness

At this moment of shared friendship and respect

Bless us all and grant us Your Peace

"Behold how good and how pleasant it is for brethren to dwell together in unity": Psalms 133:1

And so be it.

—*Olive Rose Steele*

Dear God

Thank You for waking me up this morning

Thank You for giving me today

Thank You for every new day that I see

Thank You for every new sound that I hear

Thank You for the air that I breathe

Thank You for the soft morning dew drops

Thank You for the warm sunlight

Thank You for food, shelter and clothing

Thank You for family and friends

Thank You for everyone who loves me

Thank You for a healthy, happy life

Thank You that I enjoy these blessings

Father I am thankful

Amen

—*Olive Rose Steele*

Dear God

Lord and Father of all
Teach me to be respectful of others
To be respectful of their traditions
To be respectful of their worship and praise
To be respectful of their language
To be respectful of their right to be different
To be respectful of Your Divine Spirit
Within each and every one of Your children
Give me an open and loving heart
To love as You love
And help me to be respectful of myself before
I ask others to be respectful of me
In Jesus name I pray
Amen

—*Olive Rose Steele*

Dear God

This situation makes me feel helpless

I release my opinions

I relinquish my ideas

I lay down my human will

I put aside my human planning

I give up my human ambitions

I abandon my human pride and vanity

I now give this heavy burden to You, Father

I ask You to adjust and govern this situation

Take full control of the outcome

And bless everyone involved

Amen

—*Olive Rose Steele*

Dear God

Please protect my mind from lies and negative thoughts

Help me to clearly hear Your voice over any other

Shield me from misleading and destructive thinking

Where enemy thoughts are already in my mind

Help me to push them back by inviting the power of

Your divine Holy Spirit to cleanse my thinking

Protect my thoughts from doubt and confusion

So that I can make right and proper judgments

Have mercy upon me Dear God

In Jesus Name

Amen

—*Olive Rose Steele*

Dear God

Thank you for my friends

My friends have shown me tremendous love

They support me in good and not-so-good times

They bless me with gifts I would not have asked for

Their love is nourishment in tough times

Father, I appreciate my friends for their generosity

Let me be a source of their happiness

Let me be as good a friend to them as they are to me

Bless their families

Supply their needs

May angels hover and protect all of my friends

And may my friends and I always be together

In Jesus name

Amen

—*Olive Rose Steele*

Dear God

I stand with your beloved daughter, Dorothy

the one in whom You are well pleased

I thank You for blessing her with a wonderful life

You know the number of her days

You know her purpose on this earth

You know how much you've asked her to complete

Father, keep her healthy and strong so that she may complete

Your work.

As she walks may your Angels surround her at all times

And may they protect her from harm and danger

Thank you Father that your daughter is happy, healthy and

whole; Bless her and give her a long, wholesome life

In Jesus name I pray

And so be it

—*Olive Rose Steele*

Dear God
Have mercy on my mother
She held me in her arms at birth
She nurtured me in my formative years
She gave me advice when I needed
I thank you for directing the role she played in my life
She is on her way to the place You prepared for her
Give me strength to support her on her journey
May angels watch over her and comfort her
In Jesus' name I pray
—*Olive Rose Steele*

Dear God
I am challenged by fear in its different guises
Threatened by fear from all sides
I cannot fight these terrible fears
They hinder my logical thinking
And my ability to make right decisions
Help me to know only the fear of
God, give me courage to stand my
ground, let me trust in You alone
Hold my hand through this difficulty
And give me Your peace
In Jesus Name
—*Olive Rose Steele*

Dear God

Take care of me

For my enemies have descended upon me

They enclose me with hate in their hearts

They curse and speak evil against me

Come to my defense and rescue me

Remove my foes from out of my path

Let them stumble and fall

For they mean me no good

Let my enemies hang their heads in shame

Let then not be able to look at me

Shield and protect me

From their lies and evil

For I ask these mercies in the Name of Jesus Christ

Amen

—*Olive Rose Steele*

Dear God

This situation makes me feel helpless

I release my opinions; I relinquish my ideas

I lay down my human will; I put aside my human planning

I give up my ambitions; I abandon my pride and vanity

I now give this heavy burden to you

Father, I ask you to adjust and govern this situation

Take full control of the outcome and bless everyone involved

Amen

—*Olive Rose Steele*

Dear God

I give You the contents of my heart

Purify with fire that which is unclean

Cleanse and use that which is useable

Bless me with a happy, loving and prosperous life

Enclose me with joy and total bliss

My spirit salutes the holiness in other spirits

My arms reach out in comfort to other arms

Keep me in oneness with my divine purpose

As I remain in Your service

In Jesus name I pray

—*Olive Rose Steele*

151

Dear God

My tasks are plenty

My responsibilities are heavy

Guide me back when I go off course

Show me a clearer and easier path

Give me strength to go the distance

Grant me full knowledge and understanding

That I may complete my tasks in perfect ways

Bless my coming in and my going out

Now and forever

—*Olive Rose Steele*

Creator of the universe

You give us this gift of food

To nourish us and give us life

Bless this food that you have made

And the human hands that have prepared it

May it satisfy our hunger

And in sharing it together

May we come closer to one another.

Amen

—Taken from: The Book of Alternative Services of the Anglican Church of Canada

Parting Prayer as a song

May the good Lord bless and keep you

Whether near or far away

May you find that long awaited golden day today

May your troubles all be small ones

And your fortunes ten times ten

May the good Lord bless and keep you till

we meet again

May you walk with sunlight shining and a

bluebird in every tree

May there be a silver lining back of every cloud you see

Fill your dreams with sweet tomorrows

Never mind what might have been

May the good Lord bless and keep you till we meet again

(May you walk with sunlight shining) and a bluebird in every

tree.....

—Meredith Willson, Composer.

APPENDIX I

I started to journalize my prayers, ten years ago, as a healing exercise, at a point in my life, when comfort escaped me. The place was precarious. I was hanging on to a slender thread. My prayers were my crutch. My passionate state of mind was all I presented to my Heavenly Father. And I knew then, my humble prayers were all God wanted from me. My prayer entries turned out to be a gift—a calling I would otherwise have missed. My prayers guide my spiritual walk, direct me along the way and point me to a solid ground. The entries in my prayer journal became material for my first book *And When We Pray.*

Now, I reflect on how other people may benefit from having their own prayer journals and so I designed a Section of *The Solid Rock* to encourage folks to write down their feelings and re-write them as they please.

Your own journal entries might be your spur to a true life turnaround. You will discover from your journal entries that you may not need to repeat the same supplications and mantras because God heard you the first time. You will enjoy fresh moment by moment conversations with your Heavenly Father that will move you to a place of spiritual improvement. And you will find yourself giving thanks more often.

My hope is that you'll find yourself returning to *The Solid Rock* to update your answers to the **Truth Exercise.** And as you grow and mature in your soul walk, you may change previous responses as necessary. *The Solid Rock* could very well be your book of simple explanations to your challenging questions. Having your personal copy is a fresh start to a good life. May the good Lord bless and keep you until we meet again.

APPENDIX II

Do you feel better after reading *The Solid Rock*? Will you take away information that you can use on your spiritual journey? Has *The Solid Rock* impacted your life; influenced your personal relationship and made a difference in how you see yourself in the general scheme of daily living—how you relate to others and how you view your world? Please tell others about your experience.

Think about the people you socialize with, work with and worship with; can you think of someone who needs to experience emotional healing? Spiritual healing? Give them the contact information on how to get a copy of *The Solid Rock*. We will make sure a copy of this book gets into their hands as quickly as possible—give someone the gift of words.

Reader feedback on this and my other books (And When We Pray and Great is thy Faithfulness) have indicated that I write more inspirational books. Readers told me that my books have been a positive influence in their lives; they say my books are easy to read and understand and my suggestions relate to them. I am humbled by such honesty and I will continue to write inspirational books as I'm prompted by Spirit within.

Please help me to help other folks. Think about people you know that are still drifting—looking for a compass.

Consider individuals who are seeking to change their ways of living and thinking; share the message of this simple book. Thank you.

Please check out *The View from my Coffee Cup* ... my monthly Blog, posted at WordPress at: oliverosesteele.wordpress.com.

E-mail: oliverose29@yahoo.com
www.about.me/oliverose29
www.amazon.com/e/B004W80S8W
Twitter: **@olive_steele**

AND WHEN WE PRAY:
Suggestions and Prayers for Living in Spirit
5.25" x 8" (13.335 x 20.32 cm)
Black & White on White paper
ISBN-13: 978-0981072302

Self-Help / General

And When We
Pray

Suggestions and Prayers for Living in Spirit

Olive Rose Steele

First published work by Olive Rose Steele, *And When We Pray* (Suggestions and prayers for living in Spirit) is a book of prayers and suggestions on how to deal with the challenges of day-to-day living. *And When We Pray* includes many logged prayers from Steele's prayer journal. She reveals, with honesty, her faith in prayer and encourages readers to rely on the awesome power of their prayers for every need in all aspect of life.

A review by: Cal Mandy, Mississauga, ON

Olive Steele has written a remarkable book which provides insight into her life challenges and how she rose above them. She shares with her readers her thoughts and feelings about prayer; how praying helped on her life's journey. And why we have a strong instinct to pray. The prayers she has written are honest and inspiring, giving hope that we can also overcome the difficulties we are faced with. I have been dealing with some tough problems and as I began to read the prayers they captured so perfectly what I had been feeling for so long. As I continued to read I began to feel at peace, as if I could summon the courage to change my life, because I knew I was not alone. You will find smiles and laughs in the book also. I had the good fortune to have met Olive and was inspired by her positive attitude toward life and the power of prayer, her serenity, her wisdom, her patience her sense of humor. This is a book that will be 'well worn', not just read and retired to a bookcase.

REAT IS THY FAITHFULNESS:

Insights for Seekers of Self

5.5" x 8.5" (13.97 x 21.59 cm)
Black & White on Cream paper
192 pages

ISBN-13: 978-1475150629
ISBN-10: 1475150628

Body, Mind & Spirit / Spirituality / General

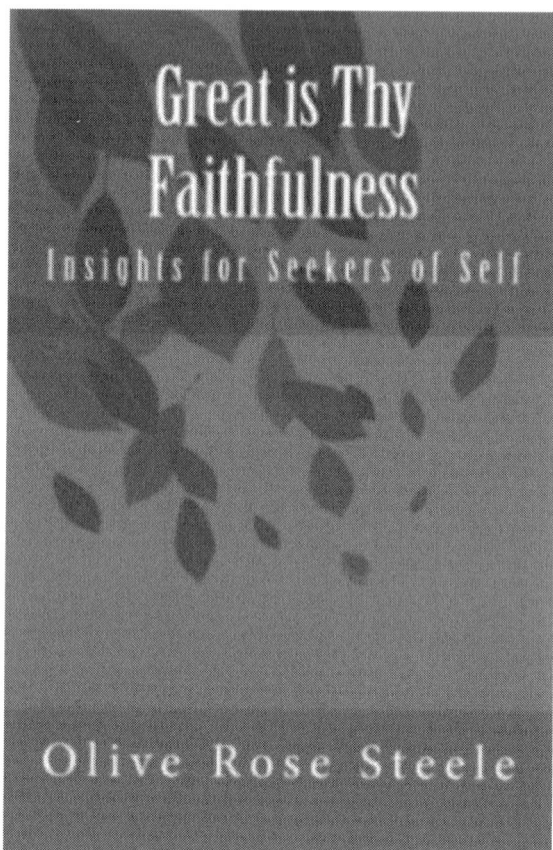

Prologue *by S.S. Laing, PhD, Psychology*

Great is Thy Faithfulness is a pointed journey around the bends and through the curves and grooves of life that is skillfully captured using simple themes, and enhanced through spiritual reflection. The many themes that the author explores and shares from her life's journey—Ego, self-belief, respect, judgment, truth-telling, ambition, authenticity, change, stillness, and acceptance—mirror the range of emotions that we all encounter in our own life journey. Her account however, is valuable because she helps us to reflect on the source and purpose of these life themes by simply calling them out, forcing a level of honesty that initially feels burdensome. She then helps us to lift the burden by offering prayer as the alternative to 'going it alone' and surprisingly, we experience levity in the midst of hard truths. To fully experience *Great is Thy Faithfulness*, one must be still, open, and willing to be reflective; this is not a 'coffee-table' piece. As you read, you will find yourself revisiting a life circumstance, reflecting on your stance to a situation, re-evaluating your interpretation and approach to handling the situation and re-organizing your experience. *Great is Thy Faithfulness* may ultimately help the reader achieve a level of honesty and acceptance about the "Is-ness" of life devoid of foreboding, and rich in clarity and buoyancy.

Cry tough

5" x 8" (12.7 x 20.32 cm)
Black & White on Cream paper
286 pages
ISBN-13: 978-0981072319
Fiction / Romance / Suspense

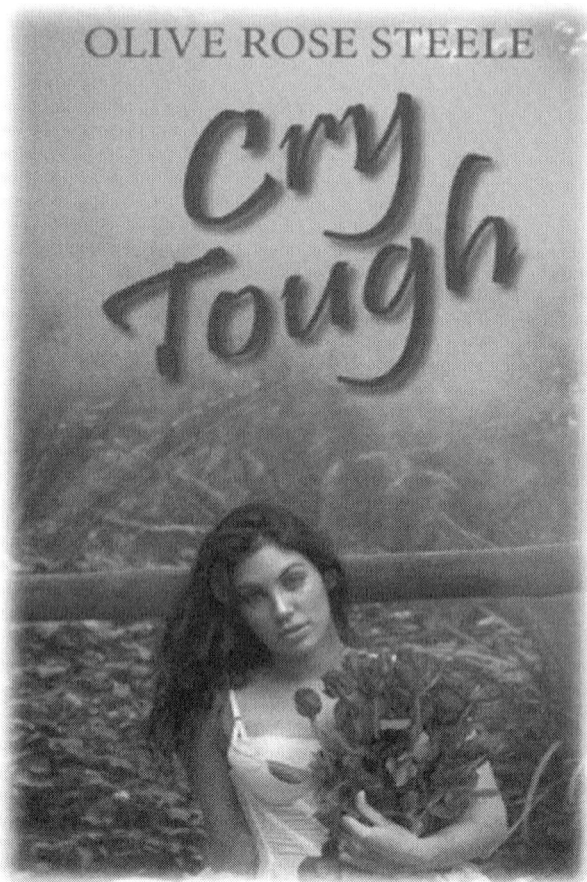

A Review by; Cheryl Antao-Xavier, Author.

In Blossom Mae Black, Olive Rose Steele has created an unforgettable heroine who evokes comparisons to one of literary fiction's most memorable characters—Scarlett O'Hara. Beautiful and brazen 'Bloss,' as she is called by those who love her in spite of her flaws and poor choices, is infuriating and endearing at the same time. If you are conservative, she will shock you. If you are a hopeless romantic, she will appeal to your heart. And if you are adventurous, prone to grab at life and ride every opportunity towards your shifting goals, well then, Bloss will get into your head and haunt you. You will want to step into her life story and make things okay. You are concerned for her. Fear for her. Want to be her and yet not want to be her. That is the strength of Steele's writing craft. Highly believable fiction. Cry Tough is a poignant story that will stay with you long after you have read through the entire novel, and reread the beginning—which is a must to bring closure to your own keening emotions—and have closed the book, and put it away.

WATT TOWN ROAD
(A Memoir)

6" x 9" (15.24 x 22.86 cm)
Black & White on Cream paper

ISBN-13: **978-1481005647**
ISBN-10: **1481005642**

INTRODUCTION

To understand my grandmother's life and even the period within which she lived, I had to go deep into *her* mother's era, if not her life. My grandmother told me little, if anything about her mother. So, I had to dig into the middle 1900s to learn about the period and the conditions under which grandmother lived. I tried to understand, in a personal way, how my fore-mothers survived. What were their hopes, fears and aspirations? How did their progress influence my background? I listened to stories told to me about my ancestors by people who had lived close to that period of time, to comprehend a civilization which was different from what I now call modern age. *Watt Town Road,* the song, was a constant refrain of my grandmother—a song, that typified her life. Be inspired by the folks on *Watt Town Road*!

ABOUT THE AUTHOR

Writing is, for Olive Rose Steele, a natural ability and a pastime she enjoys. She founded _Let's/Have/Coffee_, an informal connection that promotes and encourages inspiring conversations about the issues of life, in spontaneous settings. She blends faith and spirituality in comprehensible self–healing ways and draws on life experiences to provide inspiration. Olive Rose Steele is mother of one and grandmother of two. She lives with her husband, Herbert in Ontario, Canada.

COMING FALL 2016
BY OLIVE ROSE STEELE

WATT TOWN ROAD
(*A MEMOIR*)

Field workers retired to their cots by sundown, unless it was Friday... Storytime... when lamps in the common room flicker until midnight.

The population in Marl Ground had started to rise; two field workers, four field workers, six field workers. Each year, more female field workers were fixing to birth babies.

Then, on a quiet Sunday afternoon, just before Christmas, the population of Marl Ground jumped from 401 to 412. A stranger had arrived with his wife and nine children to settle down. They aim to start a business—a total surprise to Busha Muir, the self-appointed Mayor of Marl Ground.

04/01/2023 Elizabeth
11:00 am
Paola.—

Manufactured by Amazon.ca
Bolton, ON